ASSOCIATION PODCASTING

(TELLING YOUR ORGANIZATION'S STORY WITH AUDIO)

SECRETS FROM A PODCAST PRODUCER.

BLAKE ALTHEN

TABLE OF CONTENTS

INTRODUCTION

Human Factor (my Company) started producing podcasts in 2008. In those days, "selling" the idea of a podcast was much more difficult than it is today. The iPhone was less than a year old. Access to the Internet over the air on mobile phones was limited, expensive or both. This meant you had to go to a computer or, if you owned an Internet-capable phone or device, you had to be in WiFi range in order to download a podcast on your device of choice. More likely, you downloaded it on your computer, connected your device and transferred the file over to your device. WiFi was not everywhere, the way it is now. And on top of limited bandwidth, there was another problem: Almost no one knew what a podcast was!

Sure, people would nod their heads and pretend to know what a podcast was. But you would soon know they had no idea what you were talking about when they would say "I *watch* them here and there." Since they were so new, we literally had to teach people how to get them on their phones/pods. In the beginning, that went something like this:

1. Plug your device into your computer
2. Open iTunes
3. Go to the iTunes store
4. Search for (fill in the podcast)
5. Click "Subscribe"
6. Download the episode
7. Sync your device

8. Open your podcast app on your phone or device
9. Press "Play"

All those steps were one of the reasons podcasts struggled to become mainstream. But despite all of this, I knew that the second Internet speeds for mobile devices got faster, that podcasting would take off. But what I didn't see until a few years later was the incredible opportunity podcasting would give to membership-based organizations such as associations, unions, nonprofits and others with similar models.

Major news and entertainment companies must have a large reach. They need massive amounts of eyeballs and eardrums seeing and hearing their content to make money. They are using a revenue model of advertising which by its very nature, requires large audience to be effective. Media companies will go to potential advertisers selling them on the idea that they have, for example, "around 3 million Caucasian, married mothers between the ages of 25-34 with a median annual income of $55,000 - all tuning in to watch or listen to our content." Let's make an example of a baby food company. Media companies would approach a baby food company and tell them that they could reach exactly who they were trying to sell to on a daily basis; in the above case, that would be new mothers. And you could see how this might be very appealing to such a company. Brand awareness can be crucial when selling something to a mother feeding her baby. If Oprah says it's great, then it must be great.

So where is the opportunity in association podcasting? The answer is niche. I will use a fictional association, the Widget Makers of America (WIMA), frequently throughout this book to illustrate examples. But it doesn't have to be an association. Any organization with a membership, unions, nonprofits, NGO, etc., can benefit from this information. There may only be 10,000-30,000 widget makers in the USA. So even if a major content maker had all 30,000 that is not nearly enough to interest most major media outlets. They *might* consider it for a little exposé piece, but there are just not enough eyes and ears to justify the big production costs to make a show.

But with production costs coming down, this is where WIMA can now step in and communicate to its membership. Sure, major brands like Dove soap may not be interested in targeting the average widget maker but companies that sell the widget raw materials may be EXTREMELY interested in reaching that widget maker. Sponsorships and being associated with the industry's premier trade show or annual conference is an extremely attractive opportunity worth top dollar. If WIMA could tell a vendor that every week, for 20-25 minutes, they could reach 2,000-4,000 widget makers for 20 minutes a week that all use a product or service that they make, would that be of value to them? Of course it is.

Some organizations, PACs and NGOs for example, may not be able to accept sponsorship money from podcasts, or it may be frowned upon. So is there still an opportunity here for them? Absolutely. Having a weekly show relating to your organization's constituents and/or members can show a human side to what can sometimes be a faceless entity where one's dues go. Actually hearing about the good work - whether it be goals reached, industry news or continuing education - can make your organization seem more human, and help you connect to those people you are trying to reach on a much deeper level. You will literally be speaking directly into your target listeners' ears, when and where they want to hear it.

BUT WHAT'S THE ROI, BLAKE?

This is one of the most complex questions to answer. There is an obvious answer: sponsorship dollars. You can put advertisements before, and inside, the show. But that is not the only factor of ROI when it comes to making an amazing podcast. The next one is harder to quantify on a spreadsheet or a P&L report but is very important. I have seen many examples, both personally and with clients of what I call UROI (Unintended Return On Investment). These benefits include everything from a large member prospect becoming a member because of info they heard on an episode, to members coming up to the association after recording at a live event and expressing what the show means to them and how they listen every week, to the president of an association interviewing a celebrity influencer and having a great time, to smoothing over a very upset member who was thinking of leaving by offering them some time on the show to showcase their work. There are many more.

I can personally attest to the UROI in our own business. Some of our podcasts have produced many thousands of dollars of business. The connections we have made from both people that we have had on the show and people that have listened to show have lasted for many years and made lifelong clients for us.

One of the keys is to have a great and consistent show. Whether you want to do it all in-house or contract some or all of it out, this book is intended to help you get started on your organization's podcast journey. Enjoy!

About The Author
(The Short Version)

I have been in the production business for over 20 years. In 2001, I launched Human Factor, along with my business partner Paula Bellenoit, and we were off to the races. Since then, my team and I have worked on feature films, trailers, promos, advertisements, and more. These projects have earned me nominations for coveted awards such as Promax, Addys, JPF and Grammys. To see a full list, go to www.humanfactor.net.

We produced our first podcast for the trade association Women in Film and Video in 2008. Through that process, we began to realize that we – with our studio location in Arlington, Virginia, in the outskirts of the Nation's Capital – were sitting in the Hollywood of trade associations. We quickly learned as much as we could about associations, and began to figure out the best ways to help them tell their stories, and also how to get their stories out there, to their membership. Our client list quickly filled up with names like National Association of Convenience Stores (NACS), Footwear Distributors and Retailers of America (FDRA), American Dental Association (ADA), American Bar Association (ABA), National Retail Federation (NRF), and the list goes on and on.

Sometime in 2016, I realized that there was much more to this whole podcast thing than just recording audio; strategizing on processes, workflows, trade shows, marketing, and websites was also necessary. As a result, we began to focus on those services, specifically geared towards podcasts.

Fast forward to today, and association podcasts make up a large portion of our business at Human Factor. I have made literally THOUSANDS of shows for associations. I love applying my years of audio/visual storytelling to this mission-driven community.

If you would like the longer bio, it will be at the end of this book.

Part 1. The Pilot Process

Let's Set Some Goals And Expectations

The podcast startup phase can be daunting to an organization. Where to begin? You have so many things to think about. Who will we have on the show? Where will we record it? How long should it be? I could fill many pages with such questions. Also in my experience, some organizations can be very risk-averse. Meaning: they don't want to start something, and watch it fail two months later. The fear of failing and looking bad looms. So how do we mitigate the risk?

Here is the way I have come up to help either launch a show or test out the idea of a show. It is a three-part method we use to help guide you on whether you want to go forward with a series, without breaking the bank and wasting a ton of time.

We basically borrowed the old record label model of band demos or television's model of piloting a show. You may have noticed the first episode of a television series may simply be called "Pilot." What is a pilot? Wikipedia defines pilot as:

*"A **television pilot** (also known as a **pilot** or a **pilot episode** and sometimes marketed as a **tele-movie**) is a standalone episode of a television series that is used to sell the show to a television network.*

Television networks use pilots to discover whether an entertaining concept can be successfully realized. After seeing this sample of the proposed product, networks will then determine whether the expense of additional episodes is justified. A pilot is best thought of as a prototype of the show that is to follow, because elements often change from pilot to series. Variety estimates that only a little over a quarter of all pilots made for American television proceed to the series stage,[1] although the figure may be even lower[2]

Most pilots are never publicly screened if they fail to sell a series. If a series eventuates, pilots are usually—but not always—broadcast as the introductory episode of the series."

That is exactly what we would do with your podcast. Instead of trying to get the money and the resources to make 52 episodes, let's just make four to six and see how it goes. We have a three-part approach to this. There is a series of two meetings and one recording session:

1. The Kickoff Meeting
2. Pilot Recording day
3. "Strat Comm" - Strategic follow-up

This process is intended to give your organization a few episodes so you can determine whether you want to continue the series. It will methodically go through a checklist leading to the eventual release (if you choose to do so) of your podcast series. Of course, you will be able to modify this process if you like, as you see fit. I am simply sharing with you how we have done things with many organizations. If you follow some variation of this process, you should be able to launch a successful show. Or find out that a podcast is not for your organization without wasting a bunch of tie and money. SO LET'S DIVE IN!!

THE KICKOFF MEETING

Before we push "record", start counting the number of listeners or signing autographs, we have to get organized. There are many details, from conceptual items such as, "What will the show feel like?" right down to, "What kind of music, if any, do we want in this show?". So where do we start? ALWAYS start with the "goals" of the project. Let me explain.

If I asked the CEO of a footwear association, "If, after one year, your podcast had 10 listeners, would you continue to fund the show?", I would certainly get an eyebrow raised. When I say this during our kickoff meetings, I am usually met with confusion. "10 listeners?" Let me add one more thing: "What if I told you that those listeners were the presidents or CEO's of Nike, Reebok, KEEN, New Balance, Adidas, Puma, Allbirds, Steve Madden, and UGGS? Does a total of 10 listeners sound better to you now?". Sometimes I get a "Yes!", and sometimes I get a "No". But this is how we get the discussion rolling, as to how we are going to define success.

So what is success? That question has many different answers, and you will have to define that for yourself. With that said, here are some ways I have seen others define success. Some are very measurable, and others may take a bit of thought:

1. Number of downloads
2. Certain $ amount of sponsorship dollars
3. A better awareness from your membership of your organization's activities
4. A stronger public perception and awareness of what the organization's industry does

5. Brand awareness - your organization is literally considered the "voice" of the industry
6. Educating your membership on laws, technology, thought leadership and more
7. You may have some additional goals in mind, but the list above should get you thinking about what you want out of this effort. Be sure to set a time as to when you want these goals accomplished. We have annual meetings with our clients. I suggest you do the same, whether internally or whether you are contracting a vendor to help you make your show.

Podcasting is a marathon, not a sprint. You may get lucky and burst out of the gate with 50,000 downloads a month, if you have major celebrities affiliated with your organization, or a genius marketing staff. But in our experience, we have seen organizations grow steadily, month by month.

Lastly, on goals: it may go without saying but you need to write these goals down. We designed an elaborate checklist system using a software service called Process Street. We know exactly how many downloads every one of our shows needs per week to stay on track with the download goals we set out at our annual meeting, and you should know that number as well. That said, you don't need something overly sophisticated. However, you do need clearly articulated goals. Google Drive or even a piece of paper and put into a filing cabinet will do to start. If you published your first podcast on January 1, then track progress through the year and set a meeting for no later than December, to see if you have accomplished your goals, and to think about what you might do differently next year.

Into The Weeds (let's get down to details)

During the next part of the kickoff meeting, we have to get specific. Your podcast team will have to acquire digital assets like music options, and maybe sound effects. There will be copy to write. On top of that, we ask our clients a number of other questions that will not only get you started but help you avoid some trouble down the line. The first specific detail goes without saying.

1. The Name of the Show

Every podcast needs a name. If you are not a creative writer or a Madison Avenue ad firm this can be tricky. And it's because you will find that every clever name you try is already taken. One of the tricks we have used to aid with brainstorming is to go to a site like www.pungenerator.org. Sites like these allow you to enter a word and then spit back dozens of silly puns. So if you are with the cheese association, try Googling "cheese" and see what comes up. With that search, I got some results such as cheese wiz, cheesemonger, head cheese, and more. You could see how any of those could be made into a show name. "This is The Cheese Wiz show, brought to you by the national association of *your name here*" Sometimes we can overthink these things. There is something to be said for getting to the point. What is wrong with "The Cheese Show?" That tells the listener exactly what topic they are going to hear about. As of the writing of this book, "The Cheese Show" name is still available, which leads me to my next point.

There are a few more things to be said about finding your name. iTunes is always a great place to check for podcasts but it should not be your only place. If you are thinking of going with "The Cheese Show," check for it on Google as well. Search for "cheese show podcast" and see what comes back. Run trademark and patent searches. Although I personally believe that if you're not on iTunes, you don't really have a podcast, some people don't think that. They may only have put their show on SoundCloud, or host it on their own website. Be sure that your name does not too closely resemble another name, as there is nothing worse than brand confusion. Also, search domain.com or any domain registrar for a domain name. If "www.thecheeseshow.com" is available, BUY IT!! You may have to go with some variation (www.cshow.com or www.cheeseshow.info). Owning the domain may be important in the future. I will discuss why in later chapters.

One other thing I have seen organizations do is crowdsource the name. The concept is simple: get a modest prize, a free ticket to the convention, an Amazon gift card, maybe even a new iPad. Let your members know you have a new podcast in the works, and you need their help. They can send in their ideas for the show name. The final 3 names will get $100 gift cards. Then set up a voting website. (I quickly Googled it and found one at https://www.easypolls.net.) The winning name gets $500.00. This is a really fun way to engage your members and get a variety of names in the process that you might not have gotten otherwise.

2. The Show Description

This is the brief description under the podcast title that gives the listener/subscriber the basic info about your podcast. It should be short, sweet, and to the point. Here are a few examples below to get a sense of how some have approached the show description.

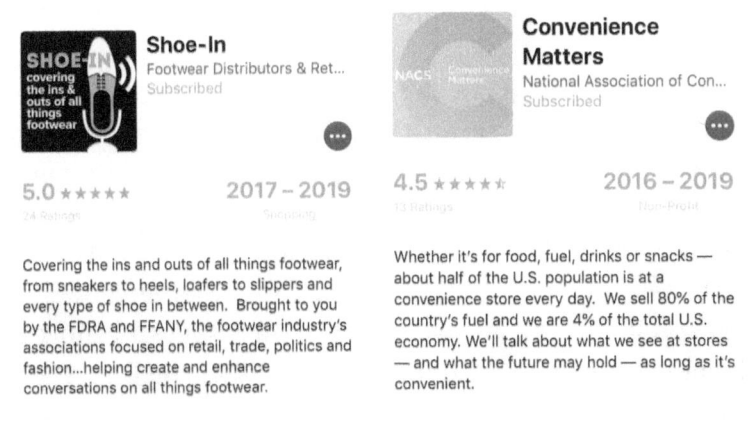

Shoe-In
Footwear Distributors & Ret...
Subscribed

5.0 ★★★★★   2017 – 2019

Covering the ins and outs of all things footwear, from sneakers to heels, loafers to slippers and every type of shoe in between. Brought to you by the FDRA and FFANY, the footwear industry's associations focused on retail, trade, politics and fashion...helping create and enhance conversations on all things footwear.

Convenience Matters
National Association of Con...
Subscribed

4.5 ★★★★⯨   2016 – 2019

Whether it's for food, fuel, drinks or snacks — about half of the U.S. population is at a convenience store every day. We sell 80% of the country's fuel and we are 4% of the total U.S. economy. We'll talk about what we see at stores — and what the future may hold — as long as it's convenient.

Hosts

Most organizations usually have a lot of ideas about who will host their podcast before they call us. Whether it be somebody in the communications department, PR, sales, marketing or government relations, this doesn't really matter. The sound of their voice, personality, and interview skills are what's important. And most of those things can and will improve over time. Also, it really helps if they want to do it. I know that may sound crazy but I have had hosts who were tasked with being hosts. It's best if the hosts are excited or at least interested in participating. But believe it or not, that is not the biggest consideration I have when finding a host.

I am more concerned with whether or not this person has the time, both in the short term and long. What I mean by this is if you have "Frank," SVP of marketing, as your host of a monthly show he may have no problem getting out of the office once a month to record a show. But do you plan to grow the show? What about at your annual event? What if the show eventually goes weekly? Can he handle that? Make sure your host can allocate enough time to be available to record the show.

I am a big fan of an anchor host. Think of Walter Cronkite or Ira Glass (The American Life). Always hearing the same voice builds familiarity and trust. Even if the entire episode is going to be presented by somebody else, I believe the open and close of the show should be consistent. It may be as simple as the anchor host recording, "Today we are going to do a special report on the new government findings on widgets. Jane Doe, take it away."

Consistency

Consistency is so important and I find with member-based organizations it is one of the most overlooked details. Shows randomly coming out during the course of a month looks both inconsistent and unprofessional. Imagine if your favorite television show just randomly appeared. There is a reason the 11:00pm news starts at 11:00pm. So when it comes to consistency, there are basically three models of shows.

- • **Monthly Show**. While I am not a big fan of the monthly show, it may be all that an organization can manage at first. In this case, I recommend you try to adhere to a regular schedule, so your audience will know when to look for it. One example of this: releasing the show on the first Monday of every month (this could obviously be the 2nd or 3rd Monday, and so on). Another example could be pairing the release of your monthly magazine or newsletter with the release of the podcast. This can be VERY effective because, with proper planning, the magazine can promote the podcast and the podcast can promote the magazine. I will talk more about synergies in later chapters.

- • **Weekly Show**. The guideline we have for this is simple. Pick a day for the release of the show and stick to it. For organizations, we have found that Mondays, Tuesdays or Wednesdays are best for this type of content. By Thursday or Friday, people are starting to get ready for the weekend, and do you really want to listen to a work-related podcast on a Friday? They are starting to go out of work mode and into weekend mode. On Monday, people are headed back to work and are in a better mindset to listen. That said, if there is a reason you think your audience would like to listen on Friday, by all means release on that day. The other benefit of a weekly show release is that you get your audience into the regular habit of listening to your podcast. Remember: consistency is key.

- • **Seasonal or Series**. You might decide to record a batch of shows, or record for a set period of time, and then take a break. This gives you the advantage of anticipating your busy times and working around them. For instance, if your annual event is in July, and you know you will have some downtime in December, your schedule may look like this:

  - o • *(WINTER SEASON) Record several episodes in December to be released in January and February.*

o • *(SPRING SEASON) Plan to record 8-10 more shows in March and release them in April and May. You may even have enough shows to release some in June.*

o • *(BREAK) In June you will be too busy preparing for your July event so don't plan any podcast work other than lining up guests for your event. (Events can be wonderful opportunities for recording shows because all of the big thought leaders are in one place.) In this scenario, that is what I will assume you have done. So in July, record 8-12 episodes on location at your event.*

o • *(SUMMER SEASON) Release your event shows in July, August and September.*

o • *(FALL SEASON) Plan to record again in September, release them in October and November.*

o • *(HOLIDAY SEASON/BREAK) In October, record just a few to get you through the holidays.*

o • *Rinse, repeat.*

What style of show should we do?

There are many ways to structure a podcast. You have interview formats, news/education formats, narrative storytelling, and blends of all three. So which is right for your organization? To start, I will say that narrative storytelling (*This American Life*, *Radiolab*) can be much harder than it sounds. Much like professional athletes, those folks make it sound easy. But having made those types of shows, I know that they can be labor intensive, more expensive to make, and require much longer lead times. On top of potentially having many interviews to record, log, and file, you then have a story arc to present and craft. Depending on who you ask, there are five, six or seven elements of a story: things like plot, setting, characters, points of view, conflict, resolution, and more. You will also have to do a fair bit of writing to properly convey your ideas. And on top of that, you will have to edit the thing.

I am not trying to dissuade you from taking on such an undertaking. But at the risk of being cliché, perhaps we should learn to walk before we try to run. Or even crawl before we can toddle. My recommendation for the beginning phases is to start with a basic interview format. Think of it in three acts:

- • Open/Setup/Tease
- • Middle/Interview/Meat
- • Close

In the *Open*, the host and co-host might have a bit of banter for 1-3 minutes on the topic that your show is going to address. It can be a current issue, some technology that is going to solve a problem, or new legislation/disruption that is coming. What we are really interested in is setting up a problem that will be answered on the show. This is to be followed by something like "We are going to answer all of these questions in this episode". The *Middle/Interview/Meat* is where you begin the conversation. We will talk more about how to get great conversations going in later chapters. Lastly, we have the *Close*. Simple statements like, "for more information go to www...; thanks for listening...; next week we will be talking about..." Also, if you know who you're having on next week's show, throw in a, "next week, we will be talking with John Doe about his thoughts on the disruption."

This basic interview format is a great place to start getting your interview skills together, without having to worry about hours of editing and pre-production.

How long will the show be?

This is a topic of much debate among podcasters. Obviously, we are not limited by a network schedule or satellite time. So anything goes. Some big-name podcasters (i.e. Joe Rogan) have shows that can go longer than three hours. Narrative shows such as *S-Town* and *Serial* may be an hour long and have multiple episodes that all connect together. They also have huge budgets and a seasoned, full-time staff working on episodes. Here is what Wikipedia has to say about attention span:

- • *Selective sustained attention,* also known as focused attention, is the level of attention that produces consistent results on a task over time. Common estimates of the attention span of healthy teenagers and adults range from 10 to 20 minutes.

Also, the average commute in the USA as of 2017 was 26.4 minutes according to the Census. This all means that I recommend that you shoot for around 20 minutes for your shows, at least in the beginning. Most likely, your membership will be listening while on the go: on the treadmill, riding the subway, driving their car, or walking somewhere. As we become better at storytelling and interviewing, we can consider a longer show, or have multiple episodes on one topic. We will discuss more on that technique later in this book.

Will there Be News Segments And/Or Stitching?

When my business partner read this book for the first time, she suggested I include this part on stitching at the end of the book, or maybe even omit it altogether. It is a tricky thing to wrap your brain around, even when explained in person; describing it in writing is even more challenging. Nonetheless, I think it can be a powerful tool, so I am going to include it. This may seem hyper-technical. Don't worry: we will get back to easier concepts in a few pages.

One of the things that organizations can consider incorporating into their show is a special segment. These can range from more formal two- to three-minute news segments, to more lighthearted "Morning Drive" type segments. I have seen various organizations employ different types. Let me give you a few examples:

The "news segment."

Before I describe how to set up a news segment I need to explain a technology call stitching. Stitching is the ability to insert markers in the timeline of your final podcast audio files. You can add an insert point or "stitch mark" into new audio files and add new audio at those mark time. So for this example let's say your podcast is always 10 minutes long and comes out weekly. Since you began the show, you have been adding stitch markers in all of your final podcast audio files, as you have been releasing them at the 5 minute mark. If you decided to run a sponsor ad in January, it would run at the 5 minute mark throughout all 52 previous episodes, if that's your plan. Then, if you decided to change the message or remove it entirely, it would update throughout the catalog of shows. You can have multiple stitch markers. They are catego-rized in three ways:

1. 1 Pre-Roll: this is a mark that plays before the show starts.
2. Mid-Roll(s): these play anywhere in the middle of the show.
3. Post-Roll: these play after the show has ended.

The reason I am bringing up stitching is because I find that for news segments, this technology can be very useful. If news is something you want to provide, even if you do it down the road, you may want to think about how to set up a show in order to anticipate markers. I am going to give you an example of how to set up a show that will have news stitching in it. It might read as follows:

VERSION 1

Music begins and fades out over announcer.

Announcer - *"Welcome to widget talk, talking all things widgets., Brought to you by the National Widget Makers Association, and sponsored by Widgettron, providing quality training to widget makers since 1995. Here are your hosts, John Doe and Jane Doe."*

John Doe - *"Welcome Welcome Welcome to the voice of widgets. The only show talking all things widgets, all the time. Jane, have you noticed that the price of widgets is going up substantially?"*

Jane Doe - *"Why yes, I have, John"*

John - *"Well, we have a great guest that is going to shed some light on why that is happening. Steve Magilicuttie is from the Institute of Widget Makers, and has written a book titled 'Widgets forever, a widget maker's life story.' Steve, thanks for coming on Widget Talk"*

Steve - *"Thanks for having me, John"*

INSERT STITCH MARK! (this is done after you record the show)

John - *"So Steve, what do you think about this new legislation on widgets?"*

Conversation begins

Now let's read this transcript of the show with the stitch inserted:

VERSION 2

Music begins and fades over announcer.

Announcer - *"Welcome to widget talk, talking all things widgets., Brought to you by the National Widget Makers Association, and sponsored by Widgettron, providing quality training to widget makers since 1995. Here are your hosts, John Doe and Jane Doe."*

John Doe - *"Welcome Welcome Welcome to the voice of widgets. The only show talking all things widgets, all the time. Jane, have you noticed that the price of widgets is going up substantially?"*

Jane Doe - *"Why yes, I have, John"*

John - *"Well, we have a great guest that is going to shed some light on why that is happening. Steve Magilicuttie is from the Institute of Widgetmakers, and has written a book titled 'Widgets forever, a widget maker's life story'. Steve, thanks for coming on Widget Talk."*

Steve - *"Thanks for having me, John."*

Stitch Plays

<u>Second announcer</u> - *"But first, here is your February widget news. Widget makers are on strike in NYC, etc, etc. New widget safety laws could greatly affect our industry, etc, etc. Lastly, Widget Con is coming up in October, and will be the biggest expo for widgets in the nation. Early Bird Registration is encouraged, so go to www.widgetshow.com and reserve your spot. Now back to the show.*

Stitch Ends

<u>John</u> - *"So Steve, what to you think about this new legislation on Widgets?"*

Conversation begins

As you can see, one really exciting thing about using stitching, is that even your older shows are getting fresh news every month. This allows older shows to be more relevant and evergreen, so that you won't have old, stale news from 2 years ago permanently embedded in it.

I want you to notice in the two variations above that, with or without the stitch inserted, the show works. If for whatever reason, you don't have news content ready, the show will play just fine without it. You want to avoid saying things like, "But first, the news" in the actual show when you record it. If you do, and the stitch doesn't appear, then you could end up with something that is very weird-sounding such as:

Host: Thanks for coming in to Widget Talk. Before we get to the guest list, we have this month's announcements. NO STITCH Steve, tell me about your work with widgets.

Likewise, you should not talk about the mid-roll stitches in your podcast. Obviously, if you talk about it, and then for whatever reason it is not there, you sound like you don't know what you are talking about.

Other types of segments

Stitching technology is ideal for more than news segments. Segments later in the show have places for them as well. Case in point: I had one trade association that had a "Quick Draw" segment at the end of their show. Basically, they asked their guest on the show some silly questions that they had to answer as quickly as possible. Questions like, "pizza or burger?", or "an app you can't live without", or "the last book you read." It was fun and light-hearted, and a nice way to end a show. I might have transcribed like so:

21:30 into the show

<u>John Doe</u> - *"Well, Steve, we are almost out of time. But before you go, we'd like for you to participate in our final segment, 'Quick Draw'."*

<u>Stitch Plays</u>

<u>Announcer</u> - *"This segment is sponsored by Widgettron, providing quality widget training since 1995. Come by booth 1398 at the Widget Show to see all of our new products. Remember Widgetron for all of your training needs".*

<u>Stitch Ends</u>

21:30 into the show

<u>John Doe</u> - *"Ok Steve, answer as quickly as possible: Coke or Pepsi".*

The reason I bring this up is because there is a slight variation to the way we recorded this segment. Notice that we started with, *"This segment is sponsored by"* instead of *"Quick Draw is sponsored by."* The reason for that is down the road we may stop doing Quick Draw. Perhaps the sergeant gets old, or we just want to freshen it up with a new segment, say, "Widget Maker of the Week." Since we don't mention the name of the segment in the stitch, it will work seamlessly for all of the shows. See what I mean:

<u>John Doe</u> - *"Well Steve, thanks again for coming in. Before we wrap up, let's get to the Widget Maker of the Week".*

Stitch Plays

<u>Announcer</u> - *"This segment is sponsored by Widgettron, providing quality widget training since 1995. Come by booth 1398 at Widget Show to see all of our new products, remember Widgettron for all of your training needs"*

Stitch Ends

<u>John Doe</u> - *"This week's member is Mary Jane, for her amazing work with..."*

Pre-Roll Stitching (opening message) can typically be used for two things:
1. Sponsorship/Advertising Messages
2. Announcements/News

Every organization can set up guidelines on how the delivery of the ads should come in. I have seen some organizations sell 30 to 60-second spots exactly no questions asked. I have also seen things be a little bit more loose on the time constraints.

Personally, I think the host reading the ads or messages is best, and it is more impactful. Hosts bring their own style and flare with the messaging. I am actually not a big fan of scripts, but rather of bullet/talking points. That said, you may have to record multiple takes of a message before it feels right. Also, sponsors may not feel comfortable not knowing exactly what you are going to say about them. On top of all that, after you submit the messaging for approval, it may get kicked back to you because they didn't like it. So be sure to manage your sponsors' expectations in this process.

One useful tip is to always start the message with something along these lines: "Hello. We will get started with Widget Talk in about 30 seconds, but first we want to tell you about Widgettron. Widgettron provides state of the art training, etc, etc."

Notice here that there is a time constraint: "We will get started with Widget Talk in *about 30 seconds*", lets people know they are at the right place, and that the message will be over in a few seconds.

The Post-Roll, (after the show) stitch is the one I have used the least often. In fact, we have only used it in one show, out of the many we have produced over the years. This organization chose to put their news at the end of the show, in the form of a Post-Roll. They had a new segment, which for the purpose of showing an example we will call, "Widgets in 90 - the Widget News in 90 seconds." In the beginning of the show, they would banter a bit and mention that the news was coming, and then proceed all the way through, to the end of the show. I realize we violated my own advice from above, but they really liked this idea despite my opposition. At the end of the show, they would thank the guest and abruptly end the show. We would time the ending with a rapid fade of the music. Then the post roll, "Widgets in 90" would start. It sounded something like this:

Music begins and fades over announcer.

Announcer - *"Welcome to Widget Talk, talking all things widgets. Brought to you by the National Widget Makers Association and sponsored by Widgettron, providing quality training to widget makers since 1995. Here are your hosts, John Doe and Jane Doe.*

John Doe - *"Welcome Welcome Welcome to the voice of widgets. The only show talking all things widgets, all the time. Of course, later on, we are going to get to the Widget News in 90, and there are some great stories coming up in that. But right now, Jane, have you noticed that the price of widgets is going up substantially?*

Jane Doe - *"Why yes, I have, John"*

Conversation continues for 18 minutes

Music begins to fade up towards the end of the show

Jane - *"We want to thank everybody for listening. Steve, where can we get more information about your book?"*

Steve - *"www.steveswidgetbook.com"*

Jane - *"Great - thanks for coming in"*

Music fades rapidly (one-second fade)

Stitch Plays

News Announcer (with new music) - *"And now it's time for Widget News in 90. In Washington, DC, something really important is happening, etc., etc., more stories. We want to thank everybody for listening to Widget Talk. For more information on us, go to etc. etc."*

As the end of this stitch plays, the music crossfades to the theme song, and we end the show.

This format does work well, but you may have spotted that there is a potential for some problematic issues. What if, for whatever reason, the post-roll stitch was not there, on a given week? You now have the host telling people that something is coming later, and it may not be there. Also, the show does end a bit oddly if there is no stitch. It just sort of...stops. Will that make or break the show? Not at all. But I always like to make clients aware of any possibilities for a flaw in the show. As of the writing of this sentence, that particular show has never had an issue. (knock on wood).

Will there be an announcer in the show open? And what should he/she say?

This is a subjective decision and unfortunately, I don't really have an objective way of evaluating whether your organization wants or needs an announcer. I can offer you this piece of advice when considering your options. The first thing the listener will hear is the music, if any, and the opening voice of the show. Judgments will be quickly made, as to what this show is about, and how professional it is. One of the reasons for having an announcer is that it is very familiar: you hear the same opening message every show. The biggest issue I have heard against having an announcer are about the same: you hear the same opening message every show. So is it a plus or a minus? Do what will work for you. My advice is this: when you record your pilots, try it both ways and see what feels right.

Will there be music? And if so, what kind - and where do we get it?

Death metal, gangster hip hop, polka, disco or silence? The opening music (or lack thereof) sets the entire mood of the show. Will the show be lighthearted, super serious, thoughtful, or something else? Perhaps a blend of feels. There are plenty of music companies out there that sell what's called production music. These are songs that are specifically designed to go behind voice-overs or in the background. Some of these companies are Warner Chappell Music, Pond 5, and (plug for me) Human Factor Post. These tracks range from $15-$500.00 depending on what song. When we assist on a music search for our clients, we ask questions like: *What should the music feel like?* We are looking for the mood, and want words like whimsical, down-to-business, technical, happy, intense, and so on. What are some songs you would like to sound like? Really...name some groups: Nirvana, Outcast, Lynyrd Skynyrd, etc.

The most important thing is **DO NOT USE POP MUSIC!** And by pop music, I mean this: If you have heard it on the radio, then you can't afford it. Yes, I know you have probably heard a low-budget podcast using a Van Halen or U2 song. You may have heard big-name podcasts using pop music. On this topic, I have a few comments.

- • Who knows, maybe they have buckets of money and got permission to use the song.
- • But - you really don't want to record 52 episodes of your podcast, and then get a "cease and desist" letter from a lawyer. Let's assume they don't want damages, but would rather have you remove all of the music, or take the shows down. That will be a total pain in the behind, and a waste of time!
- • Or - you receive a letter from a lawyer asking for money. No matter how you might want to play dumb, claim that it's fair use, or that "we didn't know," you have broken the law, period. You will lose if you go to court, and do you really want to go through all that trouble? The good news is that there are plenty of great production music that is very affordable and totally legal to use in your podcast.
- • Music companies are not interested in going after people making shows in their basements. It is bad PR, and they figure these small-time violators probably don't have any real money anyway. But theYou organization is a real entity, and the music companies might perceive that they have real money. Whether or not it's true, you'll still have to deal with their lawyers.

As for how to get a professional announcer, just head over to www.voices.com. Plan on spending $150 - $500.00. There are literally thousands of voices out there. There is no real good way to search for voice talent. You can upload some of your copy and the service will select voice talent to audition with your script. You can choose male or female and accents but honestly, you just have to listen to many voices reading your copy. You will know the voice when you hear him or her. Happy searching.

Locking In A Recording Day

This may seem like a no-brainer. But I find, especially in larger organizations, that getting the actual day set down in ink on the calendar can be a challenge. Most of the time, we will have a recording day actually worked out before this kickoff meeting. But if you don't have it worked out, now is the time. Having a "do or die" recording day makes you have to get things done and ready for the big day.

Also, if you are recording everything in-house you will need to procure all of the equipment, and have it tested and ready for that day. We will talk about the gear as well as what to look for in a studio in upcoming chapters.

Scheduling and Guests

Now that we have a recording day on the calendar, we can start inviting guests. In this scenario, I am going to assume that we are going to a studio for the day. So we will have from 9AM to 5PM to record. Your day might look something like this:

9:00 Arrive and get situated
9:15 Guest 1
10:00 Guest 2
11:00 Guest 3
12:00 Lunch (Delivery)
1:00 Guest 4
2:00 Guest 5
3:00 Guest 6
4:00 Guest 7/Solo Show

Even if you were a DJ in college you will still need some warming up. So make your first 2 guests are people with whom you are somewhat familiar. Somebody that you won't mind watching you screw up a bit. Perhaps a good member that has been around for many years and you all know very well. Or maybe somebody in the office that has a job such as a lobbyist, government affairs, or some other behind-the-scenes job, but someone that will be able to demonstrate the value of the association to the listener. These will be the people you can "warm up" on. Start trying to find your voice and rhythm.

As the day progresses, you can then invite "riskier" guests. Maybe the president of the organization or the president of the board..?? After lunch, you will be very loosened up and be able to offer a better experience for the people that may be making the decisions regarding this show. Lastly, try to do a show with no guests at all. Solo shows can be harder, because you won't have a guest to do some of the talking. You have a studio booked, time is money and eventually down the road, a guest may not show up. Being able to make the show without a guest is a great skill to have when you need it.

Album Art

It would be helpful to get a logo or artwork ready for the show. I am referring to the graphic that comes up while you are listening to a show on a device, either on your phone, mobile device or computer. As of the writing of this book, the standard size is at least 1400x1400 px. This is a square logo. Make it simple and catchy. Not too many words or faces. Remember: in the podcast stores, the picture might be as big as your thumbnail.

Meta Tag Taxonomy

In later chapters, you will see why this can be very valuable for finding shows once you have a substantial catalog. What we are talking about is defining different categories of episodes to make them easy to find later on down the road. The best way to explain this is to give an example. Let's use the example of a shoe association. The taxonomy (meaning the type of show) might be one or multiples of this list:

A. Leadership
B. Import/export taxes
C. Design
D. Athletic wear
E. Comfort wear
F. Automation
G. Sourcing
H. Manufacturing process
I. Fashion

Obviously, you will need to customize this list for your organization. And at this point, that is all you need to do. Trust me here. In later chapters, you will see why.

PART 2. HOW MUCH WORK SHOULD WE EXPECT?

There a few ways to get your content recorded, mixed and published. There are different variations on how various workflows and processes can be set up. There are subtle differences between them. But in my experience, it all boils down to three models. Within these models is where that devil in the details lurks. Here are the basic models we have seen.

Options

Model #1: You hire a production company (such as ours) to help you with just about every aspect of the show: recording the content, editing the content, mixing and finalizing the content, publishing the content. Soup to nuts.

Model #2: You record your own content, whether it be at your office, an annual meeting, or a studio. Then you hire a production company to mix, edit, and publish the content.

Model #3: You Do It All!

Model #1: Hiring A Production Company - Full Service

If you want to hire a production company to do everything, you need to be sure to pick the right one. These people will be instrumental in what your show sounds like. Like anything else, "you get what you pay for." Here are some questions you can ask to help you make your decision:

- • Where can I listen to the shows you have made?
- • How long have you been in business?
- • May we see your business license?
- • Do you have a studio? (Go visit the studio)
- How long have you been in the podcasting business?
- Can you provide referrals?

These questions should help you get a sense of the company. Have them tell you about workflows they have with other clients. Call their referrals. Ask those referrals how they like working with that company, and how the workflow is. But more importantly: ask if they know any other clients of the production company that are not on the referral list.

Another thing to clarify with the production company before you start working on a show is to be sure that your organization will own the shows. This may sound like a given. But if it isn't agreed upon up-front, you could be facing a large fee to move your show to another studio. Also, if the studio is offering to take care of hosting your show, make sure they will release your RSS feed (the file that lets you communicate with the aggregators) to you when you leave. Some hosting providers will not necessarily release the RSS feed to you. There will be more information on RSS feeds and hosting later in the book.

My company has many videos on our workflow process right on our website. In all of our proposals, we provide our business license, proof of insurance and more. We have plenty of free videos on how we work with people on all aspects of shows. Go to www.humanfactor.net

Model #2: DOING HALF THE WORK

Let's explore the second model and assume you want to record in your office. This is a scenario that can be very common. Many times associations may not be able to get a bunch of guests to a studio for the day. Or for that matter be able to allocate an entire day out of the office. So recording in their office is the best or only solution. What are our options?

A common option is to do a basic recording, and then send it to a production company to mix, finalize, and publish. We will evaluate the client's technical ability, comfort level, and provide an equipment solution (more on that to come). So where do we start? First, we need a place to record. You don't necessarily need an absolutely soundproofed room, with a glass wall, a control room, $1,000 mics, preamps, mixing consoles and more. You also don't necessarily need a degree in audio technology to get a decent basic recording done. When we outfit a client's office, we attempt to make the recording system as easy and user-friendly as possible. Let's go into some details.

First, we need a quiet room. Remember: in this option, all you have to do is record the show; no mixing or editing, etc. A production company is going to mix it, clean it up, and get it out for you. If you want to spend a little bit of money, soundproofing is always nice. If you have buckets of money, you can usually find a general contractor or soundproofing company to help you with that. Or you can go it alone. Auralux and Owen Corning are two of many companies that sell affordable soundproofing foam for offices. But honestly, we have had great results without any soundproofing at all. If you don't have space, money, or time/desire to soundproof a room, here are a few tips:

A. Try to find a room that is not symmetrical. Square and rectangle rooms reflect sound the most.

B. Try to avoid glass. Yes, I know you may want to show off that amazing view from your office or conference room. Maybe make that room-with-a-view the "green" room, or ready room. Flat surfaces such as glass or marble reflect sound, and can make your recording very "roomy" sounding.

C. Find a room with lots of "stuff." If you can find a room with a bookshelf, art, lots of chairs, decorations, etc that will help to keep those pesky audio reflections at bay.

D. Get away from where the action is. This may seem obvious. But it needs to be said. Stay away from the break room, reception area, the conference room, or that loud talker down the hall.

E. Invest in a little sign that says "RECORDING IN PROCESS, PLEASE BE QUIET." And by "invest" I mean it can be a marker on a piece of paper taped to the door. That way, people walking down the hall know to zip it.

F. In your recording room, have another sign that says "PLEASE SILENCE YOUR CELL PHONE."

Gear Options and Configurations

So now that we have found our perfect room, we need some gear. There are two methods for recording audio. You can use a hard disk recorder, or go straight to a computer. In the first scenario, we are assuming that you are recording the audio using a hard disk recorder (meaning straight to a piece of hardware, with an SD card as opposed to a computer), and then handing that off to a production company that will be doing the rest of the process to get the audio onto the distribution platforms. I will put a list of gear together first, and then explore how we can get a process together.

Basic Hard Disk recording set up:

1. Hard Disk recorder (Zoom is a trusted brand)
2. 2-5 Microphones (Shure SM7B, or Audio Technica BPHS1)
3. Headphones (Sennheiser HD280Pro)
4. Headphone Distributor (Behringer HA 400)
5. Storage for your hard disk recorder. SD card or other.
6. Microphone stands. (there are so many to choose from, Amazon is your friend)
7. Mic cables and cables to connect your headphone distributer

Obviously, model numbers and brands will come and go. So here is a basic drawing of how to set up the system:

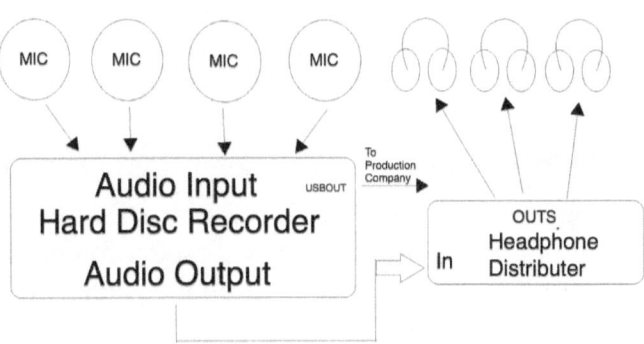

The idea of this setup is that it is super simple. Anyone - and I mean ANYONE - could sound check, push record, talk, push stop, and send it over. The reason this is so handy is that, unlike going straight to a computer, there is no need to continually update audio software, load/update drivers on a computer, learn how to export, etc. This makes your process solid, so that if someone is out sick, quits, or is on vacation, you're not stuck in a bind or locked into a key audio tech.

I have laminated step-by-step instructions for just that reason. You could put a list like this right next to the equipment. A simple workflow might look like this:

Steps to record your podcast:

1. Turn on Zoom Recorder HD6. The button is on the left side.
2. Select the mics you want to record by pushing the number of the mic on the recorder. A red light will flash when the mic is selected.
3. Set the sensitivity of the mic by speaking into each of the mics and watching the level indicator on the LED screen. Try to avoid having the mic level go into the red at the top of the meter.
4. To start recording, press the red button with the circle in it. Once you have pushed RECORD, you will see a red time code number start running.
5. When you are finished recording, press the white square "stop" button.

Steps to Upload to the Production Company:

1. Plug the USB cable of the Zoom HD6 into your computer's USB port. You will see a folder called Zoom Recordings appear in your (Finder on Mac, File Explorer on PC).
2. Production companies may have many ways for you to get them the files. At my company, Human Factor, we'll give you your own space on our web-site, "Your Upload Page," with a simple and intuitive interface where you can upload your files with just a few clicks. Most production companies have a process of delivery audio to them

3. Drag the files from the Zoom Recorder Folder onto your upload page.

4. Fill out any edit notes on the upload page. For example, *"around halfway through, we had to stop because a cell phone rang. Please edit that out."*

5. Press "complete." You're done!

As you can see, that process is ten steps. Production company systems for getting the files can vary from company to company. But for the most part, the system will be something like that.

Model #3: DOING IT ALL YOURSELF

Now that we have explored doing half the work yourself, let's talk about the last scenario, in which you want to do everything in-house. There are many ways of going about this. You can Google search "how to record a podcast" and get many results. This book is not intended to teach you how to become a DAW (Digital Audio Workstation) expert, but rather give you the basics to help you get started. So let's talk about the workflow and what you will need.

You can start with the process outlined above, and instead of uploading to a production company, simply load the files into your own DAW. However, that is one extra step you may not need to deal with. Instead, you can record straight to your DAW. The advantages of doing this are as follows.

Advantages of recording straight to a DAW on your computer:

1. You can cue music much easier.

2. Certain DAWS allow you to trigger music and voiceover cues "Welcome to The Widget Show" in real time so they don't have to be edited in later.

3. Once you're done, everything is already in your DAW and ready to edit. (You won't need to load files from your Zoom recorder, since you recorded them straight to your computer.)

4. You or your technician can mark places in your session file while you're recording, so you can quickly find spots where you might need to make edits later.

5. You can record with effects on your voice, such as EQ and compression, so it would sound a bit better as you are recording. Hard Disk Recorders can do this, however typically it is much more cumbersome to set up.

Disadvantages:

1. They can CRASH. You are running a computer and software. In my experience DAWS are not as reliable as Hard Disk Recorders. How important is that? It depends upon the situation. In the studio where you can have a "do-over," you may not worry about it, but for that celebrity guest at your convention who only has 15 minutes, I would ALWAYS use a hard disk recorder. Even if it is just a backup. Computers are always getting better but as of the writing of this book anything that is mission critical when you have no time for "do-overs" I would have a hard disc recorder set up.

2. They are more complicated, both to set up and to run. DAWs are full of buttons (on the screen of course) so there is a learning curve. You will quickly need to become very familiar with terms

like cut, paste, compress, EQ, bit depth, sample rates, monitor, hi-pass filter and more.

3. Longer set up time. This may or may not be an issue but it's worth mentioning. Adding a computer into the mix is one more thing to set up. Especially at events like conventions, where you may be running from site to site.

4. More things to troubleshoot when something goes wrong. "The mic is plugged in, but why can't I hear it from the computer?"

From a hardware perspective, they are not much different. The major difference (aside from the computer) is you will want a decent pair of speakers to mix on after you are finished. These range in price from $150.00 to as much as you want to spend. You want studio monitors, not the speakers you'd use in your living room or home theater. Call a music store or recording supplier. Some of the trusted brands are Genelec, KRK, and Mackie. The other difference is instead of a Hard Disk Recorder, you will need an audio interface. This is the device that will be converting your voices to 1's and 0's (essentially, digitizing them), and then sending them over to your DAW and then back to your speakers later. See below

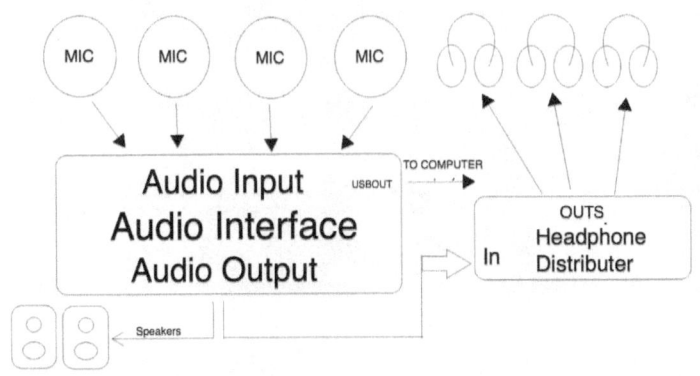

Many DAWS are similar but the recording experience can be very different, especially for the person in charge of recording. Below are some pictures of various DAW's. If pictures like the ones below intimidate you, then it is perhaps best to hire an editor/engineer or get somebody on your staff trained. If you have never used a program like these, be ready to spend some time learning.

Pro Tools

Adobe Audition

Ableton Live

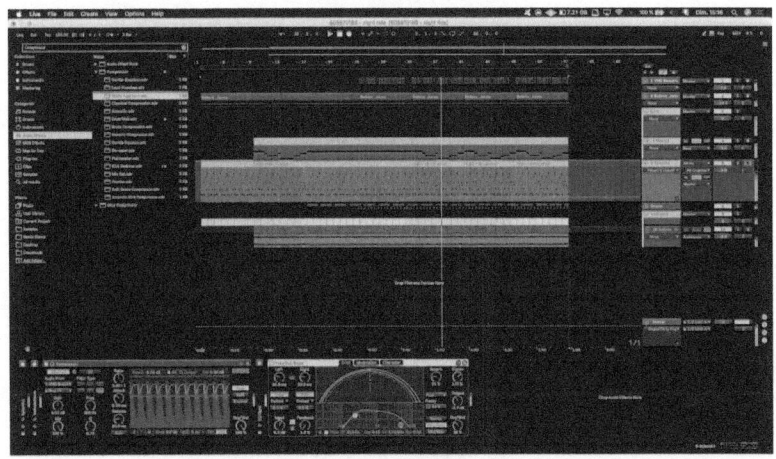

Logic Audio

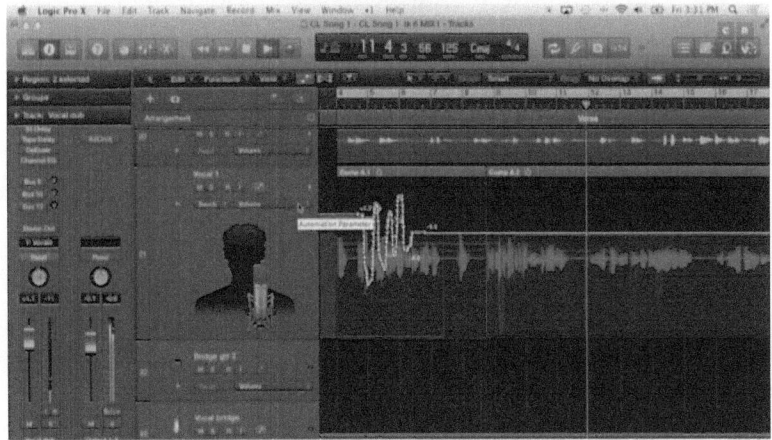

WHICH DAW SHOULD I GET?

So you've decided to go for it! Which DAW to get? Some people can get borderline religious about which DAW to use. Let me say this: in the 21st century, they are all great. Each one does things slightly differently from the others. We use just about all of them and are for the most part DAW-agnostic. It really depends on the project. But remember: we also do music, mixing, and editing in our studio. So what is right for us may not be right for you. I can already hear the haters coming out of the woodwork for the list I am about to tell you. This is just my opinion, and also based on what I have seen in the podcasting universe. My top 3 suggestions for DAW's are:

1. Pro Tools. http://www.avid.com Without question in the audio world, Pro Tools is the industry standard. Everything from podcasts to hit songs, and even feature films, are mixed and edited on it. Just about every studio in the world will have it. It can be slightly tricky to become a competent user if you have never used a DAW before. But after a few weeks, you should get the hang of it. The price ranges from $150.00 to $10,000+ (and a computer) if you want the Ferrari of DAWS.
2. Adobe Audition. www.adobe.com Tons of podcasters use this program. It is easier to use and has some wonderful audio repair tools onboard (you might have to buy those separate on other DAWs). But one of the downsides is this: if you ever want to send the files out to another studio there is no guarantee that the other studio will have it. As of this writing, Adobe is offering Audition as a subscription for $239.00/year.
3. Ableton Live www.ableton.com This software is not used by many podcasters. It is mostly a music creation software. That said, at Human Factor, we love it and use it all of the time for podcasts, for two main reasons: A. It almost NEVER crashes. You can almost try to make it crash and it just keeps chugging along. B. Clip Launch. Live has the ability to store audio clips for launch at any time. This can

be extremely useful for opening/closing music, voiceovers, segment music, sound effects, and interview clips. Unlike most other programs, you can do these things live, in real time. The learning curve is pretty different than the two DAWS mentioned above. Even experienced DAW users might find themselves thinking "huh" at times. But for a "live" sounding show - meaning you want to go straight to "tape" - it is far superior. The price point is $99.00 for the entry-level package.

I want to re-emphasize that all the DAW's today are great. If you want to try others, take a look at: Steinberg (they have Cubase and Nuendo), Motu (Mark Of the Unicorn, making Digital Performer), and Apple makes Logic Audio and Garageband which you can get in the app store for free.

GOING TO A STUDIO

If I have sufficiently scared you out of trying to do it yourself you will need to find a studio. Generally speaking, podcasts are usually not the most complex things that recording studios do. Just like with DAWS most studios are very good these days when it comes to gear. People, on the other hand, are another story. An audio tech with people skills is a must. This may sound a little flowery but you need/want a tech whose heart is in this. There are plenty of failed-musician, disgruntled audio people out there, and they can bring a recording session's energy down dramatically. So be sure your engineer has some decent manners and is good with people.

So how do we pick a studio? I am going to list some things to keep in mind when you are checking out studios:

1. Location. Does it work for everybody?
2. Can the studio handle call-ins, Zoom, Skype, etc?
3. Does the studio have an area that can be used as a "green room" or waiting room? This is helpful for the super-early guest who arrives while you're still recording a previous show.
4. Do they offer a day rate or is it only hourly?
5. Can they provide some referrals and some work they have done?
6. Do they have pictures of the rooms(s)?

Part 3. The Recording Day

So it's finally here, the big day! Since I have been in production of one kind or another since I was a kid, for me this is always the most fun. I get to see new talent come to life. I mentioned this in an earlier chapter, but I am going to mention it again. You should set up your schedule something like this:

9:00 Walk in and get situated
9:15 Guest 1
10:00 Guest 2
11:00 Guest 3
12:00 Lunch (Delivery)
1:00 Guest 4
2:00 Guest 5
3:00 Guest 6
4:00 Guest 7/Solo Show

Things to Remember

Here are some of the basic little things I like to get in, to help make the day flow better:

1. Food. This may go without saying. I typically will put out plenty of coffee, water (both sparkling and still), chips, a veggie plate, and protein bars. A nice mix of junk and healthy food. You would be surprised how many times guests (and hosts too) arrive both hungry and without any food. I am not saying that one's lunch should consist of Doritos and Power Bars, but a nourished guest

is better than a starving guest and now you're the hero. Also, you may be surprised just how fatiguing hosting a show can be.

2. Lunch. If possible, order lunch the night before. That way, you don't have to think about it the day of the recording. There are plenty of online sites such as Grub Hub that will let you do this. The lunch break is a great time to go over the things you liked and didn't like about the shows you recorded that morning so you can use what you learned when you record the post-lunch shows.

3. Opening disclaimers. There are a few things that I bring up before each show.

A. **Evergreen or not Evergreen.** PODCASTS ARE NOT ON THE AIR! Much of how we record podcasts comes from the good old days of terrestrial radio. Why do we still say "This is the Widget show?" Of course whoever just downloaded it knows that because they pushed, "Download Widget Show". In the old days, how could you possibly know what show you were listening to, without the host literally saying, "Welcome to the Widget Show." But with podcasts, you see the name of the show before you hear it. The reason we still feel compelled to announce the name of the show is purely based on habit and familiarity. Radio is live, podcasts usually are not. They are ON DEMAND. So, unless there is an emergency show, for example, short term, current news items are irrelevant. Many podcasts are evergreen (meaning you can listen to them in the future and the info is still relevant). The question then may be this: How far out into the future should a show last? That is entirely up to you, and your goals for the show which we have already outlined in the kickoff meeting. However, here are some examples of things that you rarely or never want to talk about: weather, sports scores, awards shows, etc. NOBODY CARES what the weather was 4 days ago, now matter where you live. Leave the up-to-the-minute news to live, terrestrial radio.

B. **Off Limits.** Most of the time I will ask the guests if anything is off limits. I do this for two reasons: 1) It may prevent you from derailing the show, when you ask that executive about why their membership is down, or to share prices, 2) When you do ask, "Why is your membership down?", the guest cannot get upset. You asked them if anything was off limits before the show.

C. **Set time expectations.** Tell them how long it will be. You will probably have already discussed this, but it is beneficial to state how long you expect the show to go. It also allows the guest to anticipate when it will be wrapping up.

D. **Do-Overs.** Again, podcasts are not usually live. So to save yourself some time in post-production, I recommend telling your guests that if they don't like the way they said something, or they realize that they just said something they shouldn't have, that it is best to stop in the middle of the show and start again. Maybe re-ask the question and they can re-answer it. Attempting to re-do something after the show has ended - or even worse, weeks later - is much more cumbersome then just re-doing it in the moment. Remind and reassure them that we are not streaming live, so it is no big deal. It helps them relax as well.

Show Prep

How do you prepare for the best possible show or interview? Your natural rhythm will begin to emerge after the first three episodes. If you have a co-host, your roles and strengths will become evident. Perhaps one person is good at asking the tough questions, and the other is good at opening and closing the show. I worked on a show where there were two hosts. Host #1 would research the guest in advance, and Host #2 knew absolutely nothing about the guest. This led to a nice balance, because if Host #1 and the guest got too into-the-weeds on something, Host #2 could simply say something to the extent of, "I am a bit lost, what is a.......?". Host #2 would ask the question many listeners might have wanted to ask as well.

In my experience, the guest will sometimes want a list of questions. Try to avoid sending them the questions in advance. Instead, tell them you will send them a list of topics. Even if you have the questions formed, do not send them. I've seen it more times than I'd like to count: a host will send the questions in advance, and the guest will either memorize or *actually read* the answers. There is no other way to say this: this almost ALWAYS makes for BAD CONTENT! It will sound canned, unnatural, and completely inauthentic. So here are some questions, and an example of how you could rewrite them to send to the guest:

List of your questions:
1. When was the first widget made?
2. What was your first job in the widget industry?
3. Do you think the new widget gadget is the future of widgets?

<u>Send the guest this list instead:</u>

List of topics we will talk about:

1. The history of widgets.
2. Your experience and time in the widget biz.
3. Future widget trends.

As you can see, it would be much harder to write down a canned response to that list of topics rather than questions. The conversation will be much more fluid and natural.

How many questions should you prepare?

My rule of thumb on this point: have as many questions as you like. But if a show is going to be 20-25 minutes, plan on asking three or four of them. A good podcast interview should sound like two friends having lunch, and the listener is eavesdropping on them. Conversations can go all over the place, and it is your job as a host to help guide the show, but not force it. Sure, sometimes there may be questions you feel you have to ask: like that question about why their membership is dropping. One way you might handle this is to make a segment about it: "OK listen, Mr. CEO of Widget Association: we have three burning questions the members are dying to know, are you ready to do this?". That way, it will make some sort of sense when you randomly jump from one question to the next. If you are just rifling through question after question, chances are good that the guest and listener will get fatigued, and the guest won't sound as human as you would like. In a real conversation, would you keep asking question after question? Of course no! There is a natural back and forth in real conversation. This should be no different. Don't think of this as an interview or a presentation but rather as a conversation.

The emergency question

It is always a good idea to have an extra question or two on-hand for emergencies. There will come a time when you might space out during an interview. Prepare a question that is a bit evergreen, and burned into your brain, such as, "So how did you get into the widget business?" or, "What is it that you love most about what you do in the widget business?". This can be a great lifeline when you are deep into the 4:30PM show after doing 5 episodes, and all you are thinking about is what's for dinner. Even the most seasoned professionals space out from time to time.

Pre-Interview

Some people like to have a quick call just to talk about what they are going to talk about. I think these calls should be very brief and very general. As I said before, this should be more of a conversation. When you're going to have lunch with an old friend, do you call them the night before to talk about what you're going to talk about? No! You may say "hey I need to talk to you about the new widget issue". Then you just pick a place and time to meet, and then let the conversation flow when you see each other. This is how the pre-interview call should go. Just a quick call: briefly discuss what you plan to talk about in a general sense, confirm the location and time, and that's about it.

ZIP IT!

This is something that can be a bit difficult to do, especially without a producer. Let me set up the scenario: you're in the studio, your guest has arrived, you are sitting across the table from him/her, and your tech needs you to chat so you can check the audio levels. You are both in the widget industry, so you start chatting away. Four minutes go by, and you are having a great conversation. Then the tech says, "OK you're good". Now you have to restart the whole conversation. Now you have to resay things. Or you have to say things like "like I was telling you before the show started." I know this may seem nitpicky but I believe it truly makes a difference.

There is a reason Johnny Carson, David Letterman, Howard Stern and other interviewers did not meet the guests before the show. They wanted the interviews to be totally natural. Now, they had the advantage of a green room, and a staff that can brief the guest and get them ready. My clients will be the first to confirm this: when I am the producer of a show, and I hear too much chatter before the record button is pushed, I will shut it down quickly. I usually ask them to tell me about their ride to the studio, or to count to 20, to get the audio levels set. I guess the best way I can sum this up is this: try to tell a joke twice and see how well it goes.

A Guaranteed Hit Show

Yes, I said it: there is a magic formula for a hit show!. You just need what I call my "HUB+2" formula. It's basically three things, but there are two more things that make a show even juicier. Here are the first three ingredients to the secret sauce. HUB Stands for:

1. **H**igh Stakes
2. **U**nique Circumstances
3. **B**ig Characters

The extra ingredients (the + 2) are:

1. Family Values
2. A Ticking Clock

We will get to the extras after we cover the first three. All you have to do is get about a "7 out of 10" in each of the HUB ingredients, and you will have great content. That is the good news. Here is the bad news: it's very much like exercise. I can tell you the secret to losing weight and getting a totally ripped body, how to eat right and work out properly. The problem is that this regimen can be very hard to stick to, and you have to do all of these things to achieve optimal results. So, much like exercise, following a reasonable plan can gradually lead to compounding improvement. Before you know it, you will be thinking like a podcast producer. Let's take each ingredient one by one.

HUB

1. High Stakes

If you have read this far, I am going to assume we are now friends. So I am going to give this to you straight: in the storytelling world, the highest stake is death. If you don't believe me, just turn on the 11:00pm news, or think about hit television shows. As the saying goes: "If it bleeds, it leads." That is a tall order to have on a weekly association podcast. But the good news is that the next highest stake is money. Think about any popular game show or reality TV show.

This is where the member-based podcast realm has a great advantage. Your members already have a vested interest because what you are talking about affects their livelihoods. Shows about disruption, the latest technology, a new piece of legislation and any number of other things can affect your listener's wallet. I feel like in the membership podcasts space, your high stakes will always be a 7 out of 10.

2. Unique Circumstances

There is a reason that you don't see rock concerts on television very often. Have you thought about why? When you are at a live rock show, they are great - there's loud music, the roar of the crowd, light shows, and more. But on the small screen, the experience is not the same. That said, seeing Ozzy - the prince of darkness, a legendary rock star with millions of downloads and albums sold - getting a door slammed in his face by his 14-year-old daughter is not something you see every day. We are used to seeing Ozzy in a costume, on stage with fireworks. But seeing him as a normal dad is a glimpse into a strange world, one that's not common; a world we can't access without the TV show. Pulling back the curtain if you will.

I am not suggesting you need rockstars on your show. But rather, think about what makes a unique set of circumstances in your industry. Maybe somebody who does something odd. If your industry is made up of mostly young people, try to find a senior citizen to tell their tale of working in a young person's industry, or vice versa. Another example: we were at the convenience store convention, looking for stories, and we found a company that sold bait. Yes, WORMS! Obviously, I had to try to interview him. How do you get your worms? How do you ship them? Are there different laws? Look for people that found the little secret, or have had success in odd places. Try to find the unique aspects of your industry and bring them to light.

3. Big Characters

I am not necessarily saying you need to have Dog the Bounty Hunter, Ozzy Osbourne, Donald Trump or Barack Obama to have a hit show. But we are looking for somebody with a large personality - confident, well spoken and hopefully well-known in your sector. Maybe a CEO, consultant, or president of a company, for example.

I also brought up Family Values and the Ticking Clock.

The "+2"

1. Family Values

People love to hear about family businesses, comradery, and dysfunction. Family doesn't even necessarily mean related. It could be a group of people that have worked together closely for many years. Like a group of people stuck on an island. People who have become a team.

2. Ticking Clock

This can be a bit trickier to do well on a membership podcast. Usually, when we say ticking clock we mean something to the extent of "Joe has just 30 minutes to eat 45 hot dogs, can he do it? WE WILL SEE RIGHT AFTER THE BREAK!". But you can get creative and do things like countdown to convention or time is running out for early bird renewals.

For a thought experiment, let's make up a concept for the perfect show. Here is the description:

"Today we are going to have on Lieutenant John Doe. John is the CEO of the largest widget maker in the world. He had the idea for WidgetTron right after he was shot and nearly killed while a member of the Navy's SEAL Team Six. His son and wife - his high school sweetheart - had to mortgage the house while they nursed him back to health. But their work paid off, and they went from rags to riches in just 6 short months as they changed the world of widgets. He is now warning current widget makers of why the entire industry could be at risk and why widget makers could be out of work if nothing is done about Proposition 435 Widget Regulation. Time is running out for widget makers...or is it? Welcome to the show, John."

I think you can see how that show hit them all HUB+2: high stakes, unique circumstances, big character a family values, and the ticking clock. Of course, not every show needs to be as sensationalized at that. But thinking about your shows like this can help guide your content and make it more compelling.

Steadying The Nerves

If this is your first time making a podcast, you may be a bit anxious about the first few shows. This is totally normal. Believe it or not, I need to talk briefly about alcohol, because I get asked about this more than I ever thought I would. It's probably not the best idea to drink alcohol during your shows. I have had people ask me for it, and I have seen people indulge in it. In some cases, I have seen really nervous guests have a drink, and I am OK with that. But if you are the host of a show, you need to be sharp. I have seen tipsy people think they are having a good show but when they listen the next day they are not so happy. Yes, I know there are podcasts where people smoke pot and drink throughout the show. But realistically, you are representing your organization. Let's leave the drinks for the "after party." I have produced many shows and I can tell you, everybody is somewhere along the "nervous - to - full on panic attack" scale in the beginning. But with every show, you get better and better, calmer and calmer. I wish I had a magic bullet to help calm nerves but unfortunately, the best cure is "Practice Practice Practice". Your first show will be drastically different than the tenth show and your tenth will be drastically different then you one hundredth.. Just keep doing it; you will get through it and it will gradually become easier. I PROMISE!

The Solo Show (No Guests)

Trying a show with no guests can be a great thing to practice during your pilot for a number of reasons. The first reason is fairly obvious: eventually, a guest will not show up. Things happen - car accidents, bad weather, daylight savings, kids get sick, or just miscommunications. You may still be paying for the studio time or have to get a show completed for tomorrow. "THE SHOW MUST GO ON." Not needing a guest for a good show gives you freedom.

The other reason is that YOU are the authority/voice of your industry. Why should you always have a guest? Many of the great talk show hosts never needed a guest. Whether you love them or hate them - Howard Stern, Rush Limbaugh, Opie and Anthony, The Young Turks, and Ben Shapiro, to name a few - they don't have guests on every episode. They have their own cast of characters that contribute. So maybe it's just you and your co-hosts discussing a topic.

Another trick to get the conversation rolling: go to the "mailbag", whether you really have a mailbag or not. It is good to actually ask your membership/audience about what they want to hear. As a representative of an industry or profession, you should know some of the interests and concerns of your audience. Start off the show by saying, "We have been getting tons of questions from a lot of you about the new legislation affecting widget making in China, and how that will affect members here in the USA. So we are going to get into that today. Co-host, what have you been hearing about this topic?". You have probably discussed these issues many times at the office, so why not share the conversation with the audience?

Re-Opening the Show Open

What I mean by this is simply to record the show open again, after you've finished the entire show. After you've heard the whole conversation, you can be a lot more specific on introducing the show to the listener. There are two times this can be helpful - especially with guests. Sometimes, when you are first starting out, your podcast opens can be a bit rough, to say the least. This comes more easily with practice and experience. But with a bit of editing, you can actually make the show open stellar. Let's say you originally opened the show like this:

"Welcome to Widget Talk. I am your host John Doe and today we are going to be talking all things widgets with one of the industry's foremost experts, Jane Doe. She has a degree in widgets and has recently been awarded the widget medal of excellence. Welcome to the show, Jane."

Although this show open does the trick, it is not very exciting, and does not tease the listener in a way that will incentivize them to tune in until the end of the show. But once you have recorded the show, you will know exactly what the highlights are, what you talked about, and what might be really interesting to the listener. After Jane has left you could go back and record something like:

"Hello and welcome to Widget Talk. I am your host, John Doe. You know, our industry is facing major disruption due to the new widget laws coming in the next year. One of the biggest concerns is proposition 123-ABC and how it will affect our already hurting widget supply chains. In this episode, we are going to talk to industry expert Jane Doe about three of the actual steps you can take to prevent losses at your organization. And later in the show, we will ask her what she thinks the new WidgetTron 3000 technology will mean for her business and others in the widget biz. Jane, thanks for coming on the show."

In the example above, you can see how we are not only teasing the listener as to the topic of discussion, but we are also letting them know that we are going to change subject later in the show. So if they get a little bored with one subject, they will know that we are not going to spend the entire episode on it; we will be moving on.

How to Wrap Up

This may seem like a no-brainer, but it needs to be said: if you are shooting for the 25-minute mark and we are getting towards 23 minutes, it's time to wrap up. This can be pretty straight forward. The guest will pick up on your cues. It can be a simple as:

"Well Jane, this has been so informative. We are running out of time. But in the last three minutes we have: what are the 3 key take-aways from today's conversation?" Jane will respond, then you can wrap with, "Thanks, Jane. How do people get in touch with you and your company if they would like to hire you, or want more info?". Jane replies, and then you say, "Thanks so much for joining us today. If you liked this conversation and would like to hear more, go to widgetalk.com for all of our upcoming episodes, and all of our past episodes. That's widget talk dot com."

That's a really basic way to do it. You can make it your own with a signature sign off such as "Until next week... see ya later we are outta here" or "good morning, good evening, good night" or whatever you want.

Multi-Part Episodes

You have the CEO and president of the biggest widget company in the world as your guest. The conversation is flowing, brilliant thoughts are being shared, and you know your audience is going to LOVE THIS. Then suddenly your producer signals you are at the 20-minute mark. But this can NOT end. Enter the multi-part episode.

Instead of stopping the show, just keep going. Go for 45 minutes, or until the show naturally winds down. Then the studio magic begins. Take that 45-minute interview and make it into two 22-minute episodes. You may be able to do it in one take but chances are you need to edit. Here is an example of how a show like this might sound (this is a very abbreviated version just for demonstration purposes) :

Episode Name:

Episode #45 Widget World interviews Jane Doe CEO of Widget Inc. PART 1

RECORDED AFTER THE INTERVIEW - Host: *"Welcome to Widget World. I am your host Mike Doe, and on Widget World, we talk about all things widgets. We recently sat down with Jane Doe, CEO of Widget Inc. and we had an amazing conversation. In fact, it was such a great conversation that we had to divide it into two parts. We started out by asking Jane how she developed such a passion for widgets."*

PLAY the interview edit of part 1.

After around 22 minutes - or whenever you feel it is appropriate - begin to fade up the music.

RECORDED AFTER THE INTERVIEW - Host interrupts: *"That's it for part 1. Next week we are going to resume with Jane and get her thoughts on the future of our industry. Thanks for listening."*

Episode #46 Widget World interviews Jane Doe CEO of Widget Inc. PART 2

Host: *Welcome to Widget World, I am your host Mike Doe and on Widget World we talk about all things widgets. We recently sat down with Jane Doe, CEO of Widget Inc. We had an amazing conversation. In fact, it was such a great conversation it went long enough to span over two parts. Last episode we heard all about Jane's love for widgets. If you haven't heard that episode you may want to go back to last week's episode #45. Today in part two, we are going to hear Jane's thoughts on the new disruption, laws, and how she thinks our industry will be affected by both in the future."*

Play part 2 edit. Then end the show as usual - either as you did it in the interview, or a newly recorded version.

One tip: if you have a hunch that the president of the widget company is not only thoughtful but also long-winded, then you can make a plan for this. You can plan to record the content in a certain way to have the conversation follow a flow that will be easy to split into parts. This might make life on your editor much easier.

You could then even *plan* to do two parts and actually wrap up part 1, and then begin another recording to start part 2. This way, you would not even need to do any editing. One last thing: you do not always need to keep to 25 minutes. If you believe the content is that good, then leave it at 45 minutes.

Trying out Segments

In earlier chapters, we mentioned segments or "bits." Most of the time, these have been placed at the end of the show. The best thing about an end segment is that it has the potential to hold or tease the listener until the end of the show. If in the beginning of the show, you say something to the extent of, "Welcome to the Widget Show, talking all widgets all the time. As usual, we are going to have our favorite widget gadget of the week coming up later in the show, and man-oh-man, you don't want to miss this week's favorite widget gadget of the week, it's the future of widget gadgets." Now, *that* can build excitement.

End segments can also be a great time to let your hair down and have some fun. Humanize your guest a bit more with something a little more relaxed.

Some ideas for segments are:
1. Member Highlight
2. Random fact (not topical things, just random facts about your industry)
3. Q & A from the audience (obviously you would have to set that up ahead of time or use the mailbag idea)
4. Product review of something in your industry
5. Social media fun
6. Ask the guest about their favorite book, and why
7. Rapid fire questions (just silly things as fast as possible, pizza or burgers, Coke or Pepsi)
8. Story of the Week
9. The Time Travel. Look back at an episode you have done in the past and reflect on how things have changed.

Obviously, some of these options require a catalog of shows but perhaps down the road, you can build up to doing some of these. It can also be fun to throw music under them to give them a separate feel from the rest of the show.

Remote Footage From Trade Shows and Meetings

We will discuss recording at trade shows and events in later chapters. But in the pilot phase, you can experiment with what I call "footage shows." Perhaps you have just had an event where you managed to get some footage - video or audio - of some of your thought leaders. Whether it be a speech, lecture, keynote, or break-out session; it almost doesn't matter. You can take that footage and repackage it for the podcast. I have seen this done a number of ways. To give you an idea, here is how I have incorporated this kind of footage into a show.

Go through your footage and try to find three 5-7 minute clips of people speaking on a topic that's hot - i.e. how to source materials for widget makers, the new regulations about widget making, etc. Then start the show something like this:

WENDY - "Welcome to the Widget Show talking all things widgets. I am Wendy and that's my co-host, Steve. Hi Steve."

STEVE - "Hello Wendy."

WENDY - "Steve, we all know that the widget regulations are coming next year and they are going to affect our industry big time."

STEVE - "Yep, that's for sure."

WENDY - "Well, as you know, we just had John Doe, Jane Doe, and John Johnson speak at the widget meeting, and they gave a great talk on this topic. They all had some differing opinions on what the new regs will mean. I want to play you Jane Doe's thoughts on how Prop 2345 is going to affect the widget supply chains. Have a listen."

PLAY CLIP OF JANE.

STEVE (after the clip) - "That was so interesting! I had no idea that the widget makers would be affected like that. I think that leads into what John Johnson had to say about widget automation. He had some really great insights. Take a listen."

PLAY CLIP OF JOHN.

STEVE (after the clip) - "I think we can all agree that although these automation regulations may be costly at first, but widget makers will be much safer in the end; and that could actually lead to higher profits in the industry."

WENDY - "Speaking of profits, John Doe is the president of the most profitable widget making company in the country, and he shared his thoughts on how he sees the widget industry going into the future".

PLAY CLIP OF JOHN.

STEVE (after the clip) - "Those were some amazing ideas from the meeting. Hope you enjoyed this episode of Widget Show, and hope you can make it to the expo next year in Las Vegas. This was just a sample of some of the amazing speakers we had", etc, etc.

CLOSE SHOW

What is great about these types of shows is that you are repackaging content, they don't really take that much time to produce, you can market them with your speakers' popularity, and you give the audience a glimpse of what they can expect at a conference or expo.

Finalizing the audio

Let's get a little technical for a bit. Finalizing your audio is the last step before you put your podcast out to the world. I am not going to give you a giant audio tech tutorial in this book. If you run a Google search for "finalizing audio," you will come across terms like loudness, LKFS, LUFS,

True Peak, and other geeky-sounding terms. They all refer to how "loud" your audio is. Think of it this way: if your show is too quiet, your audience will have to turn their speakers or headphones up really loud to hear your show. As speakers get louder, there is a chance that they will add noise to your show - typically a "hiss" sound. Now, you want your content to be loud enough for listeners to hear it over traffic noises outside their car, running water while doing dishes, lawnmower engines while they're doing yard work, etc. On the other hand, if your show is too loud, it will come blasting out of your listeners' speakers and could potentially sound distorted or crackly, or just completely startle your listener in a negative way.

As of the writing of this book, the standard spec Spotify is -14LKFS -2 True Peak. If you really want to understand this, just google "podcast loudness specs" and you will get more information than you know what to do with. LKFS (Loudness K-Weighted relative to Full Scale) or LUFS (Loudness Unit Full Scale) both refer to the measurement of the entire show's loudness. And True Peak is the loudest point in the show.

If you are going to be recording this yourself, you should know that in the audio geek world, 0 is the loudest, and then we go backward -1,-2,-3, etc). So according to Spotify, the loudest your show is allowed to be is -2. That said, as of the writing of this book, there are no laws that mandate this. So if your show is too loud, you won't get a fine from the FCC. But it is good to try to follow the guidelines. There are already such laws in place, for radio and television broadcasts, but none for podcasting...yet.

If you are in a studio, just ask your audio tech to deliver your final audio WAV's/MP3's at -14LKFS -2 True Peak. If you are recording this yourself, I'd recommend you go to www.izotope.com. They have many products that can both analyze and fix your audio and get it to the right spec.

Why is -14 LKFS -2 True Peak Important?

We discussed previously how effective stitching can be in making your show both current and evergreen at the same time. You're dropping new audio, whether it be news, announcements, ads, etc. in the middle of another show. Imagine that you are in the middle of the main show and you say, "and now a word from our sponsor" at -19LKFS. And then, **IN TODAY'S WIDGET NEWS, CEO OF MAJOR COMPANY PROMOTED"** comes blasting out at -10LKFS. Then, as the ad wraps up, you would get something like: **"THAT'S ALL THE NEWS THIS WEEK, SEE YA NEXT WEEK"** at -10LKFS, then "OK, so let's get back to widget talk" at -19LKFS. This would be a bad experience all around: it demonstrates a lack of professionalism, and also forces the listener to constantly grab the volume knob to turn the show up and down. Not to mention, it would probably take the listener out of the experience of enjoying one consistent show. If you are using stitches, then matching the loudness on all of your audio files is crucial to keeping a sense of continuity and consistency with your show. Lastly, it is ideal to have the loudness on all of your shows be consistent whenever possible.

A Few More Tips

Take Pictures

It's so funny how this seems like such a basic concept. But in the moment, I have to confess that even I myself am guilty of forgetting to snap some pictures. You don't need a professional photographer of course; but if you can get one, great! The more important thing is that you get creative with the picture. This is not always easy, but a little effort can go a long way. Unless you are sitting with either an A-list celebrity or one of the top 3 thought leaders in your industry, taking a picture of yourself, sitting around a table with a guest, is NOT INTERESTING. Try to get creative. For example, we had a guest on a show who was a recycling expert. After the show, we simply went and got our recycling bins right there in the studio, took the tops off them and put them around the hosts' necks (see the pic below). The picture was fun, and made the show much more "click-worthy."

**Jeff Lenard, Carolyn Schnare, NACS,
Convenience Matters Podcast**

I wish I had a silver bullet for how to make (for lack of a better word) "click bait," but there is no official formula when it comes to most member-based organization podcasts. That said, you know your industry. What gets them excited? What makes them drool or perk up? The other thing that I have found is that if you are slightly nervous with an idea for a picture, then you might be on the right track, believe it or not. I am not encouraging you to do something that will get you fired. But I remember a professional photographer friend who specializes in high-end photography telling his talent, "The weirder you feel about what I am telling you to do, the better this will be." That always stuck with me, whether it was in the music business, podcasts, photography, video, or almost any creative venture. Be creative! If you don't like it, that's what the delete button is for.

Shoot Some Video

No, you don't need hair and makeup people, two grips, or a director of photography. But a little video can go a long way. After you are done with the interview, you know what you have spoken about. You may have the guest in your studio, or you may be on location. This is a perfect time to pull out your iPhone and make a little 10-20 second video to pop on your social media outlets. You don't have to get super fancy. It can be something simple like this:

"On this episode of Widget Weekly, we are on location at the annual meeting, talking about the new widget laws with widget expert John Doe. We talked about some really important issues like X, Y, and Z. So click the link below to hear the episode or go to widgetweekly.com".

Then post that little video on your social media channels. If you really want to get fancy, you could put your theme music behind it, and end with the graphic of your show's logo. Those little touches are not necessary, but can make your video seem a bit more polished. If you have the budget for a bigger production, than give it a shot. Although I have found that keeping it simple can actually be just as powerful. Just remember one thing: the quality of the video can be less than perfect, but the audio should always be as good as possible.

Metatag the Episodes

Remember in the Kickoff Meeting we created your taxonomy (the basic list of categories that describe the main content of each of your episodes)? Now we need to use them...and all the other data that pertains to each episode. If you have a wizbang database program like Soundminer or Monkey Tools, that's great; then you obviously already have a system in place. If not, you can do it with Excel and Dropbox. Simply copy all of your pictures, session files, audio, and video into your Dropbox folders. Come up with a folder structure that works for you and STAY CONSISTENT. Then create a spreadsheet, maybe even a Google Sheet where the metadata can live. You want to track everything you can right from the start, because once you have a large catalog, this task can get unwieldy. Here's an example of some of the basics you will want to keep track of:

Of course, you may have more data you want to track. Some shows have rotating hosts, and they like to track of which ones hosted which show. Keep pictures together with their episode files. Store your episode descriptions here. Anything that is relevant to you, or that you would need if you had to recreate the episodes on another platform for whatever reason.

Part 4. The Strategic Follow Up

How to Present to the Top Brass

If you are the decision maker on this project, then you may want to skip ahead to the next section. At this point, you probably know whether you either have a viable show or will have a show with a bit more practice. If you need to sell the concept to the boss or a board, read on. If you have gotten the go-ahead to put these pilots together, that shows that there is at least some interest in releasing a podcast to the public or membership. Remember, though you have been through the wonderful creative journey, the decision makers have not. Getting the podcast packaging right can be extremely helpful in getting the podcast "sold" upstairs. What do I mean?

Presentation and packaging is important. If possible, do not send the decision makers a bunch of MP3 files. That's not a real-world scenario of how the podcast will be consumed and it does not represent what the end product could be; nor does it show the amount of work you and your team have put into this. Also, nobody listens to a podcast like that. When we present a podcast pilot to an organization after the recording day, we take great care with preparations - everything from the visuals, to when we let them hear the shows. First, let's discuss visuals. It's time to put your web design skills to good use.

The Podcast Website

But Blake, you didn't say we had to become web designers! Relax, you don't need to have a doctorate in computer science. What I am talking about is a very basic website that will be separate from your organization's website. I have had many instances where organizations are hesitant about creating a separate website for their podcast, and I will discuss that shortly. But for the time being, just go with me on this. Most member-based organizations, trade associations, unions, NGOs, etc have a bunch of content already on their main web pages. They generally dedicate separate pages or tabs for sections such as About Us, Mission, Advocacy, Foundation, Events, Continuing Education, and many more. And let's be honest: most pages need to be very official, and they should be. They represent their industry. They represent their members. But the podcast's website should tell the story of the members and the industry. To do that, you need to have even more pages. Some of the pages or sections might be related to the podcast mission, "Meet the Host", the episode catalog, upcoming live episodes, email sign up, and more. Between all of the other information found on association websites (upcoming events, advocacy issues, leadership pages, continuing education, the foundation page and much much more) the podcast can literally *get lost* in the main organization's website. So that is why we usually start with a "micro-site."

The "microsite" is a place where the listener can check out the show. It should be streamlined, and a bit more fun than the official organization's site. Also, having a microsite will allow the search engines - like Google - to have another place to find you. There will be fewer distractions on the microsite, with more focus on the show. You should only need a few pages to make this site at first. Include a handful of elements like:

1. About Widget World
2. Meet the Team
3. Episodes
4. Contact us

Those are the basics. I will go through them one at a time.

1. ### About Widget World Page

    This can be as simple or as complex as you want it to be. A sentence or two about "What Is Widget World?", with a photo of your whole team. On some of the more elaborate sites we have designed, we have added a short video highlighting the hosts speaking about the "what and why" of the podcast. This can be as fancy as a full video shoot or it can be filmed with an iPhone camera. The point is not to win an Oscar for Best Video Production, but rather to humanize the show. Allow people to see what you look like. Let people see who you are, and what your show is about. It should not be more than one to three minutes in length.

2. ### Meet the Team

    This page is where you can play around with your host. On our projects, we will show a few fun pictures with the hosts and producers of the show. Little anecdotes like favorite quotes or foods, and personal details like, "where do you vacation?" all add a nice touch. When it comes to the bio, I typically keep it in first person. Lastly, stay away from the "LinkedIn" style bio. Make it fun! Nobody really cares where you went to college. Say what you love about your work, the industry or the people you represent.

3. Episodes

This can be as simple as a list of episodes with links to the RSS feed, or as fancy as implementing that metatag database we spoke about earlier. We will talk about RSS feeds later; but basically, that is where the podcast lives. Since we have been keeping a little database about the show, you may be able to use this to create pull-down menus in the future. This may not seem like a big deal when you have six shows. But believe it or not, you will probably have 100 shows in no time. At that point, your list of episodes will be extremely long, and anyone looking for something could easily give up. See what I mean below.

4. Contact Us

   This can be as simple as "Contact Blake Althen: blake@humanfactor.net". But I think we can do better than that. Instead of the traditional Contact Us, why not try a separate page called: "Tell us what you think" or "Reach Out." This page can have a form in it.

   For this example, let's go with "Tell us what you think." This conveys much more than the old fashioned "Contact Us." Instead of a simple email field, include additional fields such as:

   A. What would you like to hear about on the show?
   B. Want to be a guest?
   C. Suggestion for a guest.
   D. Suggestion for a topic.
   E. Email Blake directly and tell him what you think.

Those are the basic pages you will want to have on a podcast's website. Even if you have to put it on your organization's main website, the same principles apply. At the very least, I strongly recommend that you obtain a private web domain i.e. www.widgetworld.com, and redirect it to the podcast area on your organization's website. A "redirect" in this case, means you will automatically send visitors on www.widgetworld.com to www.widgetassociation.org/podcast. This is extremely useful for advertising the show.

It is much easier for the host to say (and remember): "Go to www.widgetworld.com to hear more episodes" at the end of a show, than "Go to www.widgetassociation.org/news/media/podcast."

That is not an exaggeration I have seen URLs that long. Of course, if you have a web designer that wants to get creative, by all means go for it. We have found that having a separate brand identity is very helpful, and lends your podcast credibility, as opposed to just being yet another corporate initiative at an organization.

If you are not a web developer, use a service like www.squarespace.com. After a brief learning curve, it can be pretty simple and they have some great basic premade templates for podcasters.

The Big Presentation

We are ready! We have 4-7 episodes, with some captivating segments and great-sounding mixes; we have proven that we can book shows and get a month's worth of content done in 1 day; and we have a beta website ready to show. So what could possibly go wrong? In our experience, this is usually enough to get the green light to make more shows. But let me share one more thing we do, to help argue the cause a bit more.

When we present everything, we do a few things in a very specific order. If the meeting is on a Friday at 1:00 PM, we will send the audio files of the finished episodes to the decision makers the day before. We will do this in such a way that guarantees that it will be heard - whether that means we send it by email, Dropbox, WeTransfer, or burn a CD (Yes - believe it or not, for more old-school executives, I have actually burned CDs so they can listen to it in the car on the ride home). The point I am trying to make is this: you want them to listen to it, and ideally get excited about it. And you want it fresh on their minds for the next day's meeting. If you give them the show too early - let's say a week before the meeting - it will not be fresh in their minds, and the buzz may have worn off a bit.

Next is the meeting itself. Start off the meeting with a simple question: "So what did you think? Let's talk about what you liked about it first. Discuss." Then ask, "What could be done better?" Let people answer. Then say something to the extent of, "Now we would like to show you how we plan to get the word out." Depending upon the state of your mock-up site you may want to remind them that it is only a demo before you pull the site up on your conference room TV or monitor. If your microsite is not totally done, let them know it will be even better, and remind them that you value their opinion because you are really close to it and need fresh ideas. Lastly, sometimes I have found it can be helpful to have another organization's podcast site ready to show so you can give an example of what the completed job might look like.

I used to bring all kinds of stats and data on how popular podcasts are. But I don't really bother with that anymore. If you think you need it, there is no shortage of podcast listenership data out there; just search "podcast trends". I considered listing dozens of statistics in this chapter, but every organization is podcasting for different reasons. Some are doing it for continuing education or sponsorship dollars, while others may be more focused on thought leadership or public awareness; or it can be a mix of reasons.

If you have followed the steps in this book thus far, you will make an excellent case for your podcast to get the greenlight.

IT'S A GO!! NOW WHAT?

If you are the boss, and you are convinced your pilot can lead to many more amazing shows, congrats! If you are the producer, host or sound tech (or all three), and you just got the go-ahead, congrats! Call me up and invite me to happy hour so we can celebrate our hard work paying off. Relax over the weekend because we have to get back to work on Monday morning.

Now we have to get the shows out to the world. Here is our to-do list:

1. Finalize the first release day
2. Find a podcast hosting service
3. Finalize the website
4. Get the initial promotion ready
5. Get more recording dates lined up

1. Finalizing the Release Day

This is an easy enough thing to say, but it is very important. This is our deadline. All of your communications build up to this day. For that reason, give yourself a little time - perhaps two weeks (maybe more) at a minimum to plan things out. It will come extremely fast.

2. Finding a Podcast Hosting Service

You could probably write a book on hosting services alone. Let me give you the basics of what hosting is. The host will provide you an RSS Feed (Really Simple Syndication or Rich Site Summary) Think of that as where the podcast lives. All of the distribution platforms look to that for the actual content, meaning the audio and picture. There are many services and the prices range from free to hundreds of dollars a month, depending on how much bandwidth you use. It could be hundreds or even thousands of dollars if you start getting huge download numbers.

It seems like there is a new hosting service popping up every week. They all have various things that they claim to do differently. So how do you choose?

First off, ALWAYS be skeptical of "free". I know you have heard this many times, but if it is too good to be true it probably is. You know, "you get what you pay for." What is the upside of "free"? These sites can look surprisingly attractive. Many will tell you how they will monetize it for you. Some may have editing features, easy-to-read analytics and more. So what's the catch?

Quick disclaimer: I have not investigated every single free podcast hosting service in the world. So there may be some that I don't know about that are the best thing since sliced bread. Disclaimer over.

If you subscribe to a free service, there are a few things that may be serious issues for your organization. First, the ads. They have to make money somehow right? In our experience, some free hosts will run advertising during your show. Some might even pay you to do that. If you and your organization are OK with that, then it is not an issue. But imagine a scenario where you start running your own advertising, and then they stick their advertisement on, right after yours. That is a lot of ads for a 20-minute show. Not to mention that you don't even know where they are going to stick their ads.

Also imagine if you were the web developers association, and before your show they run a squarespace ad (instant website service). The optics of that could look pretty bad. It could look like you are endorsing a vendor. Again, if you are OK with that, then maybe you can use the service.

But before you sign up for the free service there is another - and in my opinion more important - issue. Who owns the RSS Feed; and if you leave your hosting service, will they transfer it to the new one? Let's paint a few scenarios.

What I am about to tell you happens more than you think. You have your amazing podcast hosted on a free hosting service. You are getting good traction. You have 9000 streams and downloads a month. Then one day you go to upload a new show and you get 404 Page Can not be found. The hosting service went out of business. What do you do? Itunes, Google Play, Stitcher, and all the other podcast players are looking to your RSS Feed to get content. But you can't upload to it. THIS IS REALLY BAD! Remember most people just check their podcast players to see if new content has gone up. Some people, myself included, rely on their podcast player of choice to let them know when there is a new episode. Let's say you use the iPhone's Apple Podcast player. It is just simply looking to your RSS Feed to see if there are any new episodes there. Guess what, now that your Podcast host has gone out of biz, you can't get content to it. So you have a few options, track down the people from the hosting company or get a new feed, which is almost the same as starting over.

How are you going to get your audience to know where your new feed is? Where they should go? Are you going to re-upload all of your previous shows to the new feed? Are you going to change the names of your podcast because now when you search for Widget Talk you will get two returns. Do you get a new show name? You have now created serious brand confusion.

One more scenario. You are hosted on a free site and again, your show is rising in popularity. You want to switch to a new service that offers the stitching service I spoke about earlier and you don't want those ads that the free hosting service is putting in. You email the hosting service and come to find out that they will not transfer the feed to you, if you hear back at all. Just like the scenario from before, you are stuck and at the mercy of the host. Again, maybe there is a free service out there that is great. Full disclosure, I am always wary of "free", especially when I don't know what's in it for them. If you really want to dive deep into this topic, search: "Owning my RSS Feed", and you will get a ton of information about this topic. Believe me, this can be very important.

Pre Scheduling

Another thing to look for in a podcast host is the ability to schedule multiple shows at the same time. As of the writing of this book most of the cheaper hosts don't offer this ability. This means that you have to post your shows when you want them to go up. So what's the problem with that? Nothing if you are incredibly organized. We like to do things in batches. We also like to go on vacation from time to time. Having the ability to set up multiple shows on a schedule to release can make your day to day management of the show much more streamlined. Imagine if EVERY Monday you have to remember to get up at 7:00AM to upload your next episode. Enter the show title, show description and artwork. After a few weeks or months, this will become a burden. Also you may want to take a vacation one day. Or your podcast person may be out sick. Or you just forget. Being able to "lock and load" your shows for the month can help with your strategic plan and make life less stressful.

Which host should you use? Of course there are many services out there and you should research which ones are right for you. In house we use both Libsyn www.libsyn.com and Blubrry www.blubrry.com. Both of these services offer decent support, have been around a long time, are still in business, and they are affordable. If you want to stitch, check out the LibsynPro account.

Part 5. Getting Ready To Release Your Podcast To The World!!

Now the launch date is set and all the elements above are coming together. What else should be happening? There are many ways to launch a podcast and though similar, no two organizations are exactly alike. Obviously I would have to talk with your organization to develop the exact right strategy. Since I can not do that from the page, I will suggest several options. You can pick and choose the ones that fit your needs and the style of your organization.

At The Convention, Meeting, Or Expo

I have seen some organizations record several episodes, then put their release on hold until their annual event. Coordinating the release of your podcast with your annual event can bring lots of awareness to your podcast right from the start. You can do a lot of marketing right at the event.

- • Place marketing and signage all around the convention center. You could use little postcards, pop-up signs, digital signage, QR codes, and anything else you can dream up.
- • Record some of your episodes in front of a live audience in a breakout room or even on the main stage.
- • Have your hosts participate in panel discussions.
- • Interview your hosts to introduce the podcast.

You are going to have breakout rooms anyway, so why not do some recording? Even if it's just one episode. One of the ways I have seen it done very efficiently is like so: Let's say you have an hour break-out starting at 12:00PM. This probably leaves you enough for two episodes at 20-25 minutes. The way I have structured this in the past is to utilize the same panel of speakers for two shows. Break the topics into two major topics: Part 1: *The State of the Widget industry*, and Part 2: *The Future of the Widget Industry*. This will leave for a natural way to go from episode Part 1 to episode Part 2. The schedule can be as follows:

11:45-11:55 SOUND CHECK

Assuming you have technicians already on site setting up the sound system, chairs, water, etc, this should be enough time for a sound check. If you are setting up your own equipment, you will need to make time for that.

11:55-12:00 WARM UP THE AUDIENCE

This is where you get to explain what is about to happen, and introduce your membership to the new show or already existing Podcast. Obviously, if you're going to take questions you need to be sure you have a mic for that, so that the questions make it on the recording.

12:00 SHOW PART 1 OF 2 GO!

Now the fun part. Record. You get to feel like a broadcast superstar. You can open the show and say, "Welcome to Widget World Live From the Las Vegas Convention Center at WidgetCon (CROWD GOES CRAZY!). We are going to do this episode in two parts. First we are going to talk about the data and how we are lobbying congress.

Then we are going to have a second part which will be on the future of widgets."

12:27 Wrap Part 1

Drink some water and reset.

12:30 Begin Part 2

"Welcome to Part 2 of Live from WidgetCon. We started off last episode talking about what's happening now in the industry. In this episode, we are going to get to what's coming in the future.

12:55 Wrap Part 2

12:56 Q&A

You can record this bit for potential later use.

Obviously, you can set up your schedule any way you want. This is just a loose model that I have seen many times and works very well for a first breakout.

Poll Your Audience

Another thing that works well: have postcards printed with questions placed on the seats of all the audience members, along with little cheap pencils. We are talking about your launch, so this time the questions are more general. Once your show is established, you'll ask different questions, but you will still do this during every event. I will list some of the questions for launch and post launch shows:

A. Do you listen to podcasts (if so, do you have a favourite)?
B. What are some topics you would like Widget World to discuss?

C. Who are some guests that you would like to have on Widget World?

D. When and where do you like to listen to Widget World?

E. Do you have a favorite episode of Widget World?

F. Would you be interested in sponsoring Widget World?

G. Would you like to be added to the Widget World mailing list?

On other little thing I have seen is the use of QR codes. QR codes are special symbols that the audience members can point their phone (in camera mode) and the phone will take action, open an app, make a contact, go to a website, etc. Make a QR code that takes the person straight to your subscribe page. You may want to make a landing page so you can track how many people got to your website via the QR code.

Put the QR code up on the big screen in your breakout room (if you have one) and mention it before and after you record. You can also put the QR code on all signage and literature. Making a QR code is not hard at all. The program I use is IQR and can be found in the Apple APP Store for under ten dollars. But if you are not on Mac just google QR code creaters and you will get a bunch of returns for apps that make the codes.

That is just the generic format for launching at your convention, expo, or any kind of live event. You can customize these concepts and make them your own.

Podcasts Under Your Door

Then there's the morning podcast under your hotel door. This may or may not be the best way to launch your podcast but it is worth mentioning for future endeavours. There was a time when, at your expo, convention, or meeting, you would find a big newsletter slid under your hotel room door every morning, with all the goings-ons of the previous day, and of the day to come. That meant that there was somebody writing feverishly to finish the copy, and a nearby printing press ready to crank those newsletters out, so someone could slide them under your door in the early hours, where they would be waiting for your enjoyment first thing in the morning.

Since the podcast could be considered a verbal newsletter, why not consider doing an annual meeting edition? Except instead of sliding it under the door, it appears on your members' phones, tablets or watches. Here is a way to do it. At 6:00PM after the first day of the event, sit down with your podcast team and record some news items that you found interesting during that day's events. Then talk about what's on "today's schedule", so morning listeners can prepare for their day. Here's a little trick that we do: you can record at 7PM on Wednesday, and then set it to release at 6:30 AM the next day. That way, it feels and looks very fresh on your members devices, and perhaps makes it seem like you are up really early, working hard for your members. Keep it short, 10-15 minutes. Just something for your attendees to listen to while they are brushing their teeth, drying their hair, and getting ready to take on the big day.

When we do the daily trade show podcast we actually make videos out of them with a multi-camera shoot. Since they are on location, they can demonstrate how you are actually on site supporting the event. Since this is not a video book, I am not going to go into how to do this, technically. But I will say that the edits are done in real time with a software called Switcher Studio using iOS and iPads. It is relatively easy to do and somewhat cost effective.

The Newsletter and Magazine

Most organizations have newsletters on a monthly, weekly, and even daily basis. The print media (including digital for our purposes) and the podcast should work as a team—one promoting the other. For the launch, have your print media start showing some behind-the-scenes of your podcasts. For some reason, people love to see behind-the-scenes. Show them with headphones, chatting away - or between shows, drinking coffee. Take some quotes from the podcast. Mention the guests you've had on the show. Obviously you should reference the newsletter or magazine during your podcast. All of the communications departments should work as a unit to help launch and promote the show..

Social Media

Believe it or not, my thoughts on social media are not much different than those on print media, with one exception. First the similarities: you basically want to do the same thing you did in your print media: constantly drip out that you are about to release this podcast. Behind the scenes photos and video - on whatever platforms you use - can be very effective, leading up to the launch. The difference with social media, however, is that you can gauge what excites people, and what does not. You can communicate back and forth and get more detailed information on not just what people are getting excited about, but who they are.

Don't Forget Your Guests

Every organization has their favorite and most effective social channels. LinkedIn may work for some people, Facebook for others, and some prefer Twitter. The point is be sure to let your guests know when their episode is released. But go above and beyond, don't just say, "Hey Jane, your episode is up". Send them the embed codes to where it is on the web, Facebook, and all the social sites you have released it on. Your guests are tapped into a whole other audience, so why not use them? We have an entire process for making sure your guests get connected the week before, the day before, and the day of the show's release. Though we have it automated it basically works like this. If the show releases on Monday then on Friday before the release they will get an email telling them that their show is going to be up Monday morning. We make the email fun, and say things like, "Be sure to make sure your private security firm is ready to handle all the paparazzi." Of course we are joking and it is evident in the email. But the more fun the overall experience is for your guests, the more likely they will send it to their social platforms. Then on Monday, they get the official release which has all of the links to their episode, which they can then pass on to their own audience.

Marathon Not a Sprint

The last thing I want to say about the launch is this: while it may be exciting, it is by no means everything, and does not make or break your show. I said earlier that podcasts are a marathon, not a sprint. Most shows gradually build followings. Week by week it will gain traction. One of the things I love about this type of show is that it can mean so much to the members. I feel like sometimes I say this and my clients shake their heads that they agree with me but they don't really get it because you are in your office and studio making shows, and you don't get to see the audience.

Their "ah-ha" moment happens when they meet somebody at an expo or event. I have seen fans of the podcast shows I have worked on basically gushing and telling the hosts how much a show means to them. You have to remember that you are talking about people's livelihoods. Sometimes when making these shows, you get caught up in the rhythm of the production. Decide on topic...set date...book guest...sit down...record the show...thank the guest, etc etc. You can lose track of just how much the show is actually helping your membership.

PART 6. THE FUTURE

Live Podcasting ("WebaCast") ("Podinair")

This whole book for the most part we have been talking about audio, and audio, and then some more audio. What I am about to share can be technically challenging to do well. But it can add some real excitement and value to your show. Also, you can have a much more interactive experience with your audience due to live chat functions on various platforms. I will tell you how we do things and then some potential ways to have work arounds that may not seem as high end but could still work just fine.

YouTube, Facebook and others have the ability to stream live video. Anybody can do it. Just check your YouTube account; you will see for yourself (google "YouTube live"). Invite a guest to your studio that is a relatively big-name thought leader in your industry. A few weeks before your recording, begin to advertise that you are going to have this person(s) on your LIVE podcast and you will be talking about the hottest topics of the day. You can promote on whatever channels are effective for your organization. *Tuesday at 2:00 Eastern we will be talking with John Doe of WidgetTron about his thoughts on the widget legislation that is coming. Go to* www.widgetshow.com *to register to see the live show and participate.*

The technology required to stream to YouTube or Facebook can be as simple or as complex as you like. You could simply grab a web camera on Amazon for $35.00, plug it into a laptop and point it at yourself while you record. On the other extreme, you could buy 4 cameras, a lighting rig, a video switcher, and everything else you might need to do a full-on video production. There are plenty of resources online about how to stream video and as I said, you can expect to spend as much (or as little) as you want to get this done - whatever level of quality you think is right for your organization. The live podcast once a month can be a fun and exciting media to play with and can be very interactive because it can have a chat function so the viewers can ask questions.

Google News and Alexa Flash Briefings

As of the writing of the book the Amazon Alexa Flash Briefing is still in its infancy and very few associations are adopting it. But that will change rapidly. It is no secret that voice commands are coming. Tech companies are spending billions on things such as Alexa, Google Home, and SIRI. So what is a Flash Briefing? Let me explain why I am positive this is another form of communication that associations will be utilizing in 5-10 years.

In short, a Flash Briefing is an audio newsletter. Imagine you are in the widget business. You wake up in the morning, stretch, put on your slippers, go over to make your coffee and while you wait for the coffee to brew, you call out into the air, "Alexa, play my Flash Briefing." A little two-inch computer somewhere then responds, "John, here is your Flash Briefing from the National Association of Widget Makers, brought to you by WidgetTron, the makers of the new WidgetProduct. To find out more about WidetTron go to WidgetTron.com." And then your pre-recorded news blurb comes on, "In widget news, lawmakers announced a new regula-tion...etc etc"

There is one more really exciting piece to this content. The end of the new can say, "For more information about these stories and all things widget, ask Alexa to play WidgetMakers Podcast."

A Flash Briefing is a short news piece, up to ten minutes, that will quickly play on Alexa. Google has something similar called Google News. They are designed to run at least weekly but are more effective daily. Essentially they are an audio newsletter of sorts.

I had a client ask me if we thought Flash Briefings would replace podcasts. To this I think the answer is "No". A podcast is to a Flash Briefing what the magazine is to the newsletter. They each have their purpose and can actually work together very nicely when done right. For Flash Briefings, we have worked very hard on creating systems of tech and workflow for our clients because unlike a podcast, Flash Briefings are every weekday. I recommend if you are not going to work with a production company partner on the project, make sure you have worked out plans for how you will accomplish your Flash Briefing. People calling in sick and going on vacation can cause disruptions in your consistency.

Final Thought

I hope you have enjoyed reading this book as much as I have enjoyed writing it. Writing it has actually made me think about why we do the things we do in helping membership-based organizations pilot, launch and maintain their shows. I hope it will help you come up with the best way to get your show made.

I have many resources for you on our website at www.humanfactor.net under *Blake's Banter About Podcasts.* There you can find thoughts about podcasting, Flash Briefings and more - both technically and creatively.

One final request: If you do make a show and manage to get it to launch, please share it with me. My email is blake@humanfactor.net.

Good luck with your show!

The Last Bit About Me

In the beginning of the book, I promised to give you the long version of my history, and how I fell into podcasting. Here is the full story.

So who the heck am I, and why should you listen to what I have to say about podcasting for member-based organizations? To sum it all up, audio content has been my life since I was 10. I was always tinkering with guitar amps, soundboards and local bands. Yes, I went to band camp.

Berklee College of Music came after that. Berklee prepared me for my first job in production, working in the Washington, D.C. area as an "AV guy." I pretty much dove into anything I could get my hands on - music concerts, fashion shows, trade shows, hotel AV and festivals. You name it - if there was a sound, video, lights or a projection system, I might have been the guy behind the bunch of flashing lights, or pulling a cable.

Needless to say, the live events industry has some long hours, and until you get high up, the pay is not much to speak of. Based on my experience, I managed to land a job with a prestigious high-end AV integrator. This is where my technical knowledge quickly ramped up. I started out as the low man on the totem pole but rapidly moved up. So much so, that I got an offer from a government contractor, and found myself working AV in flight simulators for the Air Force, Navy, and the UAE. Really high-end stuff.

But alas, something was always missing. The tech challenges were good, but I soon came to realize that content was what I was missing in my life. Even though I was still playing music in my spare time, it was not enough. Then one day, the opportunity came along for me to go full time into music. I quit my safe government contracting job and went for it.

Music led me to composing, producing bands, and mixing music and audio for television. I worked with Discovery, History, A&E, Viacom, and a bunch more. I got to work with people from all over the world, and traveled to far-away lands.

At some point in the mid-2000s, I heard about this podcasting thing. Long story short: after listening to a few, I was hooked. I had to start my own. But how to get credibility?

It just so happened that my business partner in our young production company was the VP for the association Women In Film and Video. One day, while listening to her talk about a communications issue, I had an idea that went like this: we wanted to experiment with podcasting, and Women in Film needed a podcast (at least that's how I sold it to them.) In return for creative and production services at no cost, they would promote it to their list of members. A win-win situation, right? They agreed, and our first podcast was born.

Needless to say, audio storytelling was much harder than I thought. Funny anecdote: our very first podcast featured a producer from the old show "The Sports Machine." Our tech was a three-mic system with one of the mics over a cell phone. Our first shows were terrible, but we learned and grew fast. Our music business was also growing, so we managed to get our first studio in Arlington, VA right outside Washington, DC.

One day, the phone rang and it was a production colleague of mine. He told me that one of his association clients was looking to start a podcast, and he recalled that we did just that. He asked if he could refer them to us. We said "Sure" and didn't think much about it. I didn't really have a good feel for associations or of their vital importance to their members. I soon found out was that the association employees and members are REALLY into their industry. It was fascinating. Were all of these associations like this? I had to know more.

With a bit of research, I realized that unbeknownst to me, I was sitting in the Hollywood of trade associations. And all of their mission statements included communicating with their membership, the general public, legislators and more. And what better way to do that than a podcast? Could there be a business model here?

I became obsessed with learning everything I could about how these organizations work. I went to - and continue to attend - ASAE (Association for Association Executives) events, became familiar with association trends, and made a few association podcasts. The work paid off, and pretty soon we had a nice roster of amazing clients in many different sectors of the economy.

There is one major difference between the association world and network television world. I could take everything I learned at one association and apply it to another and vice versa. With TV networks, I had to sign non-disclosure agreements; but associations would even offer to help other associations. This allowed our production quality to compound. What I mean by that is I could say to one group, "Hey, the guys at the widget association are trying this idea, maybe you should try it. Here is their number - maybe call them up and see what you think." I wouldn't even dream of doing that in TV. Pretty soon we were going to conventions, shooting videos, editing videos, publishing websites and now we are an Alexa developer for Flash Briefings.

Another nice thing is that association podcasts have a reason to exist. They are, and should be, the voice of their industry; and a podcast is not only an amazing tool with which to communicate... it is an *essential* one.

We love making shows for member-based organizations. We have clients from organizations with a staff of two, some with 600 employees, and everything in between. We find that though they may not move at the speed, or have the budgets, of the network television or media companies, they are an incredibly driven, passionate bunch of folks. I say this all the time and some people may not believe me. I am honored that these organizations put their trust in us to make podcasts for their members. Thanks for reading and I hope you enjoyed this book.

Blake Althen

Acknowledgements:

Written By Blake Althen

Editing (in this order):

      Paula Bellenoit

      Kimberly Cregan

      William Althen (My Dad)

Cover Art by Amy Emam

Back Cover Text Edit Aline Althen